BigYes
LittleYes
HealthyMaybe

A new framework
for evangelism

MARK GREENWOOD

Mark is a gift to us. A seasoned and highly effective evangelist, communicator and trusted practitioner, he knows what local church leaders and local churches are grappling with when it comes to evangelism. When someone like Mark says we need to rethink our approach to helping people around us become fully committed to Jesus, I think we should listen.

This book offers a fresh scorecard for local church engagement with the people we live amongst. It is less of a methodology and more of a pathway. Mark suggests we go on a journey with not-yet-persuaded people. He suggests a process-based approach that takes seriously the challenges, sensitivities and demands of a culture and generation that have stopped responding to traditional evangelistic approaches.

He invites us to courageously begin a fresh adventure in mission which allows those he calls the "healthy maybes" the opportunity and space to discover Christ. He encourages us to walk with them and to value their every small movement on the journey towards Jesus.

Don't just enjoy this book, engage with it. It will inspire and resource you as you seek to share the "still good news" of the gospel.

Revd Chris Cartwright
General Superintendent of Elim Churches

Having spent over thirty years in the trenches, Mark Greenwood has produced a process that will help us personally and communally think through our efforts to preach Christ faithfully in an ever-changing culture. His journey metaphor is a real service to the church and I'm going to be reading the book with my leaders here at All Souls.

Rico Tice
Co-author of Christianity Explored and Associate Minister at All Souls Church, Langham Place

BigYes
LittleYes
HealthyMaybe

Challenging, practical and inspiring. This book is an absolute must read for anyone wanting to share the gospel.

Gavin Calver
Director of Mission, Evangelical Alliance

There are few people as well placed, after decades of frontline ministry, than the little fire-starter that is Mark Greenwood to speak into the church of Jesus and encourage us to go out in his name. This is a timely book which literally has the potential to change lives and impact communities.

Andy Hawthorne OBE
The Message Trust

It was in 1975 that Wheaton professor Dr James F. Engel (1934–2016) first published his now famous scale ("Engel's scale") designed to show that everyone is in a particular place be it near or far in relation to God. His point was we should acknowledge and celebrate movement towards conversion and not just conversion itself.

Big Yes, Little Yes, Healthy Maybe is the first time I've encountered this principle written up and expounded upon as a practitioners' guide and Mark Greenwood has done a great service in providing this. Mark's book is clear, fun, inspiring and full of practical wisdom gleaned from years of faithful ministry – I heartily commend it.

Revd Greg Downes
Dean of the Wesley Centre for Missional Engagement, Wycliffe Hall, Oxford

When it comes to evangelism, Mark Greenwood is a true practitioner. That's why this book demands our attention. I believe Big Yes, Little Yes, Healthy Maybe is one of the most useful books on evangelism written in our lifetime.

Mark Ritchie
International Evangelist

Mark Greenwood is the real deal. His wealth of knowledge, expertise and experience in evangelism is having a genuine influence in the UK evangelism church scene. Having experience of speaking to both adults and young people, I recognise the need to understand the journey of faith and that is so critical for this generation. In this book Mark gives us the language to articulate the importance of journey. The idea he presents through "big yes, little yes, healthy maybe" has helped me present the gospel to a wide range of audiences and in one-on-one conversations. This book is incredible, insightful and evokes a response. That response is one of passion for the lost. Everyone needs to read this book.

Grace Wheeler
Head of Evangelism, Youth for Christ

Many books have a nugget of gold but Mark's book is a wheelbarrow load! Grounded in his wealth of experience and presented with a real humility, this resource will help us as individuals and as churches to give people an opportunity to start a journey of faith. His passion for Jesus is infectious and I'm already drawing on ideas from this book as I help churches share Jesus with their communities.

Andy Frost
Director of Share Jesus International

This book is the culmination of years of wisdom and experience gleaned from the ministry of Mark Greenwood. When others have detoured into pastoral ministry, Mark has stayed true to his call as an evangelist. Fresh, comprehensive, considered and thought provoking, this book challenges some outdated paradigms around mission. I highly recommend it to every reader.

Bishop Mike Royal
Co Chief Executive, Cinnamon Network

Any book that helps scaredy Christians like me share our faith a little better gets a thumbs up from me. This one's an absolute belter.

Steve Legg
Editor, *Sorted* magazine

Mark's experience, insight, wisdom, love for people and gifting as an evangelist shine through this book. His framework for helping people journey towards Christ is powerful and will help churches redefine their approach to evangelism with clarity and impact. I've seen this material work itself out in my own church and its impact has been stunning.

Carl Beech
CEO The Edge, President CVM and Senior Leader of Redeemer King Church

Mark's style of personal reflection and practical implications over four decades of evangelism and evangelistic ministry is a journey that he invites us into, where he encourages the journey of faith and recognises that the process of people coming to faith is often around baby steps, rather than a massive sign of commitment.

The principle based out of Galatians 4:19 recognises the pains of child birth as the process of evangelism. Where we recognise that sometimes, to quote, "the morning sickness principle doesn't always look like progress, but new life is growing and a seed has been planted". This is an insightful, practical and realistic guide in the journey of evangelism and faith. I encourage you to take the ride.

Roy Crowne
HOPE Together Executive Director

We all love it when we hear stories of people committing their lives to Christ. It always gets the biggest cheer when preachers tell of people who have found Jesus and experienced his life-transforming power!

And it's certainly worth celebrating what Mark calls the "Big Yes". But he reminds us that if we're not careful we can put such a big focus on a person committing their life to Christ that we end up not celebrating all the little decisions along the way. I love the phrase he coins, the "healthy maybe". The truth is that many people, perhaps the majority, are at the "maybe" phase. This is a huge opportunity for the church, but one we may not get quite so excited about.

The charity I lead focuses on that stage. We engage with people in the community who share an interest in the well-being of their neighbourhoods. We bring people of "goodwill" together to address social issues.

We help churches connect with organisations and agencies in order to meet community needs. Time and time again we have seen unchurched people change their previously negative perception of the church and soften towards the gospel. It's time for us to address the "healthy maybe" and create conditions to make that possible.

Debra Green OBE
Founding Director of ROC

Most people don't become Christians in one huge leap. It takes time – sometimes lots of time. Mark's book helps us see our part in this long journey. God wants to include us all in his mission, but it takes patience and grace. As you read this book, I hope you'll find renewed confidence in God for your friends and family.

Neil Hudson
Director of Church Relations, London Institute for Contemporary Christianity (LICC)

Mark Greenwood has been a friend and inspiration to me for eleven years. Every time we connect he downloads some fresh, relevant and practical stuff in relation to evangelism and has helped me share Jesus with thousands of people in a better way. When he first mentioned "Big Yes, Little Yes, Healthy Maybe" to me in 2016, I thought it was genius and I was challenged at how many people I have overlooked while only chasing the Big Yes. I first heard the term "game-changer" when Bill Clinton used it to address the Good Friday Agreement in Northern Ireland. I don't use it often but I can think of no better term for this book. It will sharpen your evangelism and I am convinced putting these lessons into action will make heaven more full and hell more empty.

Mitch
Crown Jesus Ministries, Northern Ireland

Dedication

This book is dedicated to Brian Hardaker and Godfrey Fearn who knocked on the door of my home and, as a result, my whole family became Christians. Though the night had been tough you said, 'One more house,' and behind that door was the story of God at work and lives to be transformed. Thank you for obeying the Great Commission. Thanks for all that you did to make disciples of me and my family.

CONTENTS

Foreword 15

Preface 19

PART

Introduction 23

Chapter 1:
But it Doesn't Work 29

Chapter 2:
Journey – Not Just a Buzz Word 55

Chapter 3:
The Big Yes 85

Chapter 4:
The Little Yes 95

Chapter 5:
The Healthy Maybe 109

PART

Introduction 123

Chapter 6:
Using BYLYHM in Local Church Evangelism 127

Chapter 7:
Using BYLYHM in Community Engagement 145

Chapter 8:
Using BYLYHM in Church Planting 161

Chapter 9:
Using BYLYHM in Talks 171

Chapter 10:
Using BYLYHM in Personal Faith-sharing 187

Final Thoughts: Matthew's Mathematics 215

Endnotes 220

Resources 222

Acknowledgements 224

Foreword

There is a hilarious video on YouTube of two millennial youngsters trying – and spectacularly failing – to operate one of the rotary dial phones that people used for much of the twentieth century without thinking. It is a tiny reminder of a major feature of our time: much that was taken for granted yesterday is incomprehensible today.

This principle applies in evangelism. Proclaiming the gospel is never easy because human beings have always preferred either to ignore their spiritual need or to pretend they can answer it by their own efforts. But the rapid changes in our culture have made the task of evangelism harder. So until a few decades ago, at least within the so-called Christian West, if you wanted to share the gospel with someone you could generally assume they had some idea of the basic issues involved. People, by and large, knew that there was a good God, that they had fallen short of his demands and that, somehow, the answer involved Jesus. Indeed, in the past – and certainly in the UK – if you heard that someone had "got religion" you could take it for granted that what they had acquired was one of many forms of Christianity. Now if someone "gets religion" what they have started to follow could be anything from Animism to Zoroastrianism. And, of course, there are many people now throughout the West who are not outside religion, but have a religious faith that is not Christianity.

This change poses challenges to evangelism. Only a few decades ago it seems to me that you could think of people as having, jumbled up but laid out before them in their minds, the jigsaw pieces of the gospel. The task of the evangelist was to show people how those pieces fitted together and to let them put the bits into the picture. So, it was not uncommon for a man or woman to walk into a church or an evangelistic meeting and hear a single gospel message of twenty minutes and, through the working of the Holy Spirit, find that the jigsaw pieces had come together and they had come to a saving faith in Christ. Today's seekers – if they can even be called that – are now a long way further back. They either do not have all the pieces of the jigsaw or, if they do, many of those pieces are upside down or back to front. Yes, there are still those for whom the picture comes together spectacularly in the course of a short talk or sermon but, for most people, assembling the gospel picture is a far longer and more complex process than it was.

The result is that it is, or seems to be, harder than ever to proclaim the good news. This is a problem not just for those outside the church but for those inside it. It's a rule that a failure to proclaim the good news is bad news. You see evangelism is one of those things that inevitably becomes part of a virtuous circle. Churches and individuals who engage in active evangelism get to see conversions and the changed lives that are a result. Nothing encourages evangelism more than seeing that it works. On the other hand, if churches and individuals do not do evangelism, they do not see people coming to faith, and because they do not see conversions and their fruit, they come to believe that either evangelism does not work or, if it does, it is not really that important. The sad but inevitable result is that there are many people and churches who, while they may believe in evangelism in theory, do not actually do it in practice. In Matthew 13:12 we read the words of Jesus: "Whoever has will be given more, and they will have an abundance. Whoever does not have, even what they have will be taken from them." Evangelism is one of many areas of life where that rule applies. Use it or lose it.

So, as individuals and churches, we need to do evangelism but how, in this turbulent twenty-first century, are we to best do it? There is certainly no shortage of people offering advice but who are we to listen to? I would suggest that to guide us with evangelism in this brave new world we need three things: expertise, discernment and encouragement. I am delighted to say that all three of these are to be found in this thoughtful and thought-provoking book by my good friend Mark Greenwood.

Why is *expertise* important? Now, in theory, evangelism should be the most natural of things: the natural outworking of a living, loving relationship with Christ. There is a neat witticism around today: what do you say to someone to find out if they have the latest, greatest smartphone? Answer: you do not need to say anything because they will tell you anyway. And so, in theory, it should be with evangelism. It is very significant that nowhere in the letters of the New Testament is there any teaching on how to *do* evangelism: Paul, Peter and John simply assume that is what their hearers are already doing. Yet there are aspects to evangelism that can be learnt. There are good ways of doing it and sadly there are some ways that are probably completely counter-productive.

Whose expertise do we follow? There is certainly a lot of academic discussion about evangelism and much of it is valuable. Indeed, some fascinating information from research is found in this book. Yet evangelism cannot easily be reduced to theoretical elements or mathematical principles. In the effective preaching of the gospel the psychological, the social and the spiritual all come together in a way that is never the same twice. As with learning to drive, getting married or successfully emigrating, we would prefer to be given advice by someone who has done what they are advocating. We pay most attention to teachers who have walked the talk. Here in this book we are very fortunate because Mark is a great practitioner with a long track record of successful and fruitful evangelism. Let me put it bluntly: this man knows what he is talking about and is worth listening to.

Expertise, then, is essential to guide us but so is *discernment*. Discernment I take to be the skill of recognising and balancing all the issues involved in some particular situation. For Christians discernment is not simply an intellectual skill, but also involves a sensitivity to the wisdom of the Bible and the guidance of the Holy Spirit. Discernment is certainly needed in evangelism. What are we going to say to effectively bring men and women to Christ? Different voices are heard. So there are those who suggest that all that is needed for evangelism to succeed today is that the old gospel simply be preached longer and louder. There are others who suggest that the way forward is to reformulate the traditional message of repentance and faith in keeping with modern psychology and sensibilities of our age. Still others suggest that we talk a lot less and do a lot more. The question with all these suggestions is whether we are being faithful both to the message we have been entrusted with and to those we are preaching to.

Here in this book you will read about Mark's own solution, his *Big Yes, Little Yes, Healthy Maybe* or BYLYHM approach. Here while you seek (and accept with joy) those who make an outright and immediate decision for Christ (the "Big Yes"), you also encourage those who make the more cautious response of deciding to explore further (the "Little Yes") and welcome those whose response is no more than "keeping the door open" (the "Healthy Maybe"). This fits with my own experience and here, and in many other areas that Mark touches on, I sense a wise and godly thoughtfulness, refined over long years of being an evangelist.

So, we need expertise and discernment but I would suggest that we also need *encouragement*. Here I am afraid that there has been much in the way of bad practice. Aware of the need to boost evangelism, many ministers and books have used the stick of guilt rather than the carrot of encouragement. Christians are told that it is their obligation to evangelise and that failure to do so is to fall short of proper discipleship. In my own view, the result of this is a guilt-driven evangelism in which Christian witness becomes a joyless, unhappy chore. In fact, such evangelism is probably counter-productive. Those hearing such people can probably easily detect the truth that while they are sharing they may refer to the gospel as "good news" it certainly does not appear to be that for them. Pressure is a poor motivator for effective evangelism.

What we do need is encouragement and that is something that this book has. It is full of psychological encouragement, spiritual encouragement and simple down-to-earth practical encouragement. If you are fed up with being nagged into witness, please read this.

You probably gather, then, that I am enthusiastic about this book. Evangelism remains a challenge but we have no doubt made it harder than it really is. Read this book, ponder it, pray over your response, and then go and sow the gospel and introduce your world to Jesus. And what a privilege it is to do that.

J.John
Revd Canon
Canonjjohn.com

Preface

In June 1982 something happened that would change the world forever. It was in the working-class city of Bradford and the house was number seven. Two-thirds of the street had been covered over with tarmac many years before but the bottom third still showed the cobbles of a bygone era.

He approached the door, I'm sure with some trepidation, not really knowing what was behind, and still being fairly new to it himself. It had been a tough night with not many people really interested but Brian Hardaker, along with Godfrey Fearn, decided they would visit one more house in the hope that there would be someone inside who would be interested in God. Little did they know that behind this door God had been working in the lives of the Greenwood family of West Bowling, Bradford 5.

Rewind to about four years previous to this and my dad was sub-aqua diving in Eilat in the Red Sea. This was his hobby and he had been a diving and training officer of the Queensbury branch (in the north of England) of the British Sub-Aqua Club. On this trip his best friend had died from a heart attack whilst diving. As the military hospital cut off his wet suit and announced there was nothing they could do for him, my dad went outside and, with understandable deep sadness, began to think that there had to be more to life than this. This was a key point as up to then he had classed himself as a lazy atheist – he didn't believe there was a God but didn't really want to look into it; it wasn't on his agenda. Of course, this tragic event suddenly left him with the sense that surely there is more than being born, dying, and then not many people remembering you after the years had passed. Sometime after this, Mum said to Dad, "Don't you feel sometimes that something is missing?"

So why did that night in June 1982 change the world forever? Okay, it may seem a bit like "delusions of grandeur", I give you that, but the truth is when Brian and Godfrey nearly went home because the night doing door-to-door evangelism had been discouraging evangelism, God had another plan. Little did they know that God was working in the lives of the family at number seven. They didn't know that the twelve-year-old boy who was in the middle of a six-week grounding would become a national evangelist. They didn't know about the thousands upon thousands of people who would become Christians as a result. They didn't know that he would go on to become the head of evangelism for a denomination. They didn't realise that he would write books and magazines that would equip tens of thousands of Christians, and evangelistic resources that would impact countless numbers of people who weren't Christians. They didn't know that the dad of the household would become a man of prayer and an elder in a church. They didn't know that the mum would become an amazing one-to-one evangelist. They didn't realise that this mum and dad would still be going onto the rough estates of inner-city Bradford with Teen Challenge, even into their seventies and eighties, working with some of the most deprived people. (By the way, I think my mum and dad are genuine legends.) I love the saying "big doors swing on small hinges" and this is most definitely true, in a spiritual as well as a physical sense.

I hope that as you read this book you will be inspired again to believe that "the harvest is plentiful" (Matthew 9:37) and that when we start to actively look we find out where God is at work. You just never know what story you will write as you share your faith with someone – you will change the world for the better.

PART

1

INTRODUCTION

I've tried to keep abreast of culture, intentionally reading and studying to try to understand how we tick as humans – it's a subject that has always fascinated me.

Very early on in my evangelistic ministry I became aware of 1 Chronicles 12:23–38, where David was choosing people for his army. In particular verse 32 stood out to me. It reads, "Men of Issachar, who understood the times and knew what Israel should do." It struck me that it's one thing knowing what's happening around me but an entirely different thing to know what to do.

As a result of this verse I prayed a prayer to God in those early days which I still pray today: "Lord, help me not just to be shaped by current thinking on evangelism but help me to shape current thinking on evangelism." There was a prayerful desire ignited in me to do everything in my power to understand the world I was in and how I share the gospel accordingly and equip Christians to do the same.

I love the late John Stott's superb book *I Believe in Preaching* – it's still a great read for today. He basically encouraged the reader to preach with the Bible in one hand and the newspaper in the other. I read this book around the same time as I read about the men of Issachar, which was whilst I was having my training as an evangelist with OAC Ministries (formerly known as Open Air Campaigners). They enabled me to preach on the street, learning how to talk about life and to talk about faith, resulting in being able to hold a crowd of unbelievers as we explained the gospel. This was and is the foundation of my evangelistic preaching to this day.

In recent times I've heard part of verse 32 quoted a lot more: "we need men (people) of Issachar who understand the times". The last bit has often been missed out but for me I don't just want to understand the times – that simply makes me a cultural analyst. I want and believe that we can also know what we should do as the last bit of the verse says. Don't get me wrong; this isn't the easiest thing. I find it a tension many a time: where is the fine line between relevance and compromise? But we must seek to understand the times and also ask God to help us know what we must do as culture changes rapidly.

The church has changed its view on evangelism, conversion and preaching and I've tried to consider where as an evangelist I position myself – how do I become/stay culturally relevant in my speaking and yet remain biblically true? I don't want to throw any baby out with any bath water; my concern is so often that we can end up changing completely when we didn't need to.

I've seen the role of preaching being diminished and the large-scale evangelistic events being challenged. I've seen the swing away from words towards actions and a current swinging back to the centre, which I am happy with because we have always needed both and, sadly, at various times we have leaned more towards one. For me we need clear communication in words, outward demonstration in loving actions and all of this through the power of the Holy Spirit.

I have always believed and am confident of the power of the gospel. I still believe it's the power of God to salvation. Interestingly, when Paul wrote Romans 1:16 it was in a place where the gospel had not been preached, but he was still confident of its power! Are we seeing a lack of power in today's culture?

One of the areas that I have most carried a passion for is trying to understand the process behind which people come to faith i.e. just how does the gospel process itself in a person's life? It's in this context that the inspiration for the content of this book was born!

For many years I would preach evangelistically, going only for first-time commitments and never really being satisfied with how I helped those who were not ready to say "yes" to God and yet they were not actually saying "no". Much of what I share in Part Two of this book was prayerfully driven as a result of this dissatisfaction. I knew I shouldn't stop giving the opportunity for first-time commitments but how could I resolve the tension on my heart and mind?

I've become more convinced that God moves more often in the small than he does the big. Actually for me this is not a new thing but rather how he has always worked, and I'm getting a fresh understanding of that which is inspiring me more about the power of the gospel. I am more confident of the gospel and preach it with greater excitement than ever. Not all that we see visually lasts and, conversely, not all that God is doing do we see.

If we don't understand the process behind which people come to faith we can't really inform the pathway to them becoming disciples. We've always seen discipleship as the phase that kicks in post a person's decision. Difficulties arise because we don't fully realise what they understand about the decision an individual has made. For me the journey to discipleship starts before they become Christians.

There has been a lot of critique about large-scale missions or evangelistic outreaches that claim to see hundreds of people respond to the gospel but that it doesn't convert to "bums on seats". I will say a bit more about this later in the book but at this stage I would like to suggest that responding to the gospel does not necessarily mean they have become Christians. So, is the mission worth doing? In my opinion, 100 per cent yes. Sometimes when people hear the gospel powerfully and clearly communicated they feel something of God's love and presence and they respond to that.

Someone saying "yes" publicly may not necessarily mean they fully understand what they are doing. I have to say, the day I became a Christian I did not fully understand what I was doing but the longer I've stayed on the journey the more I understand what I did, and the significance of it. In strong evangelistic moments when people are invited to say yes they may in reality be saying a "healthy maybe" or a "little yes". The problem is we then don't understand why they aren't growing. For me the more people respond the better, whatever the level of their response. Why? Because I believe it's a journey and as with all journeys there are moments of decision (and indecision) along the way. We need to be willing to change our view of how people must respond.

I believe that though where we are at culturally there seems to be less awareness of Christianity – I'm actually more excited not less. We have a blank canvas to paint on and we don't need to detangle the religious knowledge that many had in previous generations. My prayer as you read this book is that you will feel the same.

Very early on, my evangelistic gifting was sharpened. I was a butcher in an old Victorian market in Bradford along with twenty other butchers' stalls and a whole bunch of fishmongers and fruit and veg stalls, delicatessens, etc. I remember having many stand-up debates with the butchers around me. My boss was agnostic and the other member of our staff was atheist. I loved the great conversations we had. Even back then I was aware of the fact that so many people made decisions about Christianity without really looking into it. I remember saying to one of the butchers, "But you don't even know anything about it, how can you say it's not for you?"

When I left my job as a butcher in 1988 to go full-time into evangelism, my boss was really kind and told me that if it didn't work out then my job was always there for me. He said, "I know you won't be back because this is what you were born for." He wasn't a Christian!

I've had a long and varied ministry in evangelism. I've done everything from door-to-door and street work. I used to speak in sixty schools twice a term in Bradford as well as speaking at mid-week youth and kids' clubs. I've spoken in some of the largest concert halls and theatres in the UK and I've spoken in some of the smallest venues too. I've spoken in churches, universities, clubs and pubs, restaurants and coffee shops, prisons and even on a ship. I could go on. Suffice to say I've probably done most forms of evangelism (I've not loved them all!) and I am thankful to God for every opportunity to in some way present something about him to those who don't know him.

Very early on in my ministry I remember making appeals and saying, "If you aren't saying 'yes' to God, you are saying 'no'." I cringe at my naivety.

It wasn't that long before I began to carry a passion to implore people just to "look closer", to "have a proper look". My first ever attempt at Christian literature was a leaflet called "Is it possible that…?" where I just wanted people to be open-minded. Of course I longed for people to meet Christ but I began to realise there was a whole journey that people needed to go through.

As my ministry began to develop I got involved in cross city evangelism in Bradford where I was living. We did tent missions called "God in the Park" in four venues across Bradford. Then we moved into St George's Hall which was the biggest venue in the city centre. For several nights the place was packed with about nineteen hundred people as we preached the gospel. By now I was doing less street and schools work and I was beginning to work with churches. My diary was full of events as I began to develop the ideas of "A Season of Mission" in local churches. I served on the ministry team of a number of churches heading up evangelism. It was during this period that I began to develop a culture of evangelism in churches around the UK as well as in my home church.

In the past ten years I felt dissatisfaction with simply giving people the opportunity to only say "yes". I didn't want or feel the need to minimise the opportunity for people to become Christians; quite the opposite, I wanted to see that increase. What I did want to do, however, was to value the small movement people make on the journey towards Christ. All this has shaped who I am and what I do today.

As I step into my fourth decade of full-time evangelism I remain ever committed to staying as fresh as I possibly can. I am more excited about evangelism than ever and I remain more committed to the message of the gospel than ever. This is for one simple reason: I am more convinced of the fact that the gospel is the power of God unto salvation than I ever have been. I have seen it changing people's lives for decades. However, I am more convinced than ever that the Holy Spirit moves more in the small than he does in the big and this is most accurately observed in the journey of faith.

As you read through this book I trust and pray that you will gain things that will help you as you reach others with the wonderful message that has changed us.

#WeCan'tCreateSoulsButWeCanCreateJourney

1

But it Doesn't Work

Have you ever been excited by the thought of getting something new? I'm not very patient at waiting and so by the time I get it my joy is explosive. Oh the disappointment when you discover it's broken.

So often we manage to motivate our churches about evangelism and then when things don't go according to (our) plan a noticeable discouragement sets in, confirming what we already thought: evangelism doesn't work. When we add to that the negative press and the current marginalisation of Christians in the public place, we have a deflated church with a losing mentality. We have a lack of confidence in the gospel and we think it doesn't work. But do you know what? I have to say that's not my experience. I think one of the problems we have is that we listen to the media headlines and how the church is "shrinking" and we never hear a different narrative.

It is true that we see a lot of people leaving the institution of the church but that doesn't mean they are leaving God or "backsliding" as we used to call it. Now I can hear the chants already, but let me just say I believe in the local church one hundred per cent but increasingly we have a fair amount of people who we have called "de-churched". These are people who have fallen out with the traditional model of church or have been hurt by the people running it. They have held onto their faith in God but they have lost their faith in church. Often what I find is when a new church plants in an area, many of the de-churched/hurt-by-church find new life in the church plant, though of course it would also be true that there would be many who don't.

Talking Jesus Research

I am so glad that my friends at the Evangelical Alliance and HOPE Together, along with the Church of England, wanted to tell a different story. They didn't do it anecdotally or by putting some spin on an otherwise dreadful situation through clever reasoning. They did it with data from genuine research. This was realised and it told us an encouraging story.

The following section is taken from the Talking Jesus survey results and is used with permission. You can download the full report by visiting **talkingjesus.org/research/** (you will also find a number of helpful resources there). The research shows a more encouraging landscape that evangelism does work but we do need to think differently about how we do it.

"What do people in England know and believe about Jesus? What do they really think of us, his followers? Are we talking about Jesus enough? And when we are, are we drawing people closer towards him, or pushing them further away?" These are just some of the questions we at the Church of England, Evangelical Alliance and HOPE commissioned Barna Group and ComRes to ask on our behalf. But this was not just for curiosity's sake. We were believing, hoping and praying that this study – the first of its kind – would be a major catalyst for effective and focused evangelism in the years to come.

The Background

It all began in March 2015, when we gathered more than forty key leaders of denominations and networks, as well as key influencers from across the spectrum of the English church. For twenty-four hours, we prayed and we talked. We shared our heart for mission; our collective longing to see God move in this nation. We reflected on an initial piece of research about adults in England, which we had commissioned Barna to undertake. The results of this first piece of research were shocking.

As we talked and prayed together, we reflected on how the power of the Holy Spirit was needed alongside the hard work of contextualising the gospel: not an institutional response but a people movement; something simple that enabled Christians to have millions more sensitive, positive, culturally-relevant conversations about Jesus that could be deeply effective in evangelism.

There are rare moments in church history where the unity of God's people is tangible. This was one of those moments. Aware that this piece of research had the potential to equip every Christian to have these Jesus conversations, denominational leaders agreed to fund further, more comprehensive research. We released the adult "Talking Jesus" report in September 2015. And since then, Christians and church leaders across the country have been unpacking the findings together, reflecting on the challenges and opportunities for sharing Jesus today. Here is a summary of that research.

Aware of the impact of the adult research, the HOPE Revolution Partnership commissioned ComRes to conduct similar research into the views and experiences of 11- to 18-year-olds (the HOPE Revolution Partnership includes HOPE, Soul Survivor, Youth for Christ, The Message Trust, Urban Saints, PAIS, Limitless, the Church of England and Tearfund). These youth findings are released in this report, offering an encouraging insight into how many young people are sharing their faith, and how teenagers are responding to conversations about Jesus.

In presenting these youth findings alongside the adult results, we can see some of the unique challenges and opportunities before us, as we seek to equip the next generation to talk about Jesus and reach out to their friends, family and acquaintances. And we've also dug deeper into some interesting differences between white British and black and minority ethnic (BME) respondents.

We believe this research will continue to inspire and encourage Christians up and down the country to make Jesus known through their everyday interactions and conversations with people.

And we continue to be excited about this unique opportunity to understand the landscape we are in – aware that this is not a quick-fix strategy but a long-term commitment to changing the story in our nation, so that people might meet Jesus, love him and follow him.

The Adult Research

The adult research was carried out in 2015 by Barna Group and ComRes. Barna Group is a visionary research and resource company located in Ventura, California. Started in 1984, the firm is widely considered to be a leading research organisation focused on the intersection of faith and culture. ComRes is a market research consultancy operating in the United Kingdom and internationally. Established in 2003 as Communicate Research Ltd, ComRes was founded to bridge the gap between communications strategy and traditional market research.

The researchers designed an online survey to administer among a carefully screened sample of 2,545 English adults aged 18 and older who were nationally representative by age, gender, region and socio-economic grade. The sample error on this survey was plus or minus 1.9 percentage points at the 95 per cent confidence level. Additional data was collected through an online survey among an oversample of 1,497 practising Christians in England. The sample error on the oversample data was plus or minus 2.5

percentage points at the 95 per cent confidence level. The definition of "practising Christian" has been revisited since the 2015 report was issued, and the data in this report uses a tighter definition (see below).

The Youth Research

ComRes interviewed 2,000 people, aged 11–18 online between 7th and 19th December 2016. Data was weighted to be representative of this audience by age, gender and region.

For consistency, respondents were recruited using equivalent online panels to those used in similar studies of adults, and parents of young people in this age group were asked whether they and their children were happy for their child to participate. This established equivalent methodology and rigour to enable comparison with similar research among adults, while also gaining access and consent.

Key findings of the survey

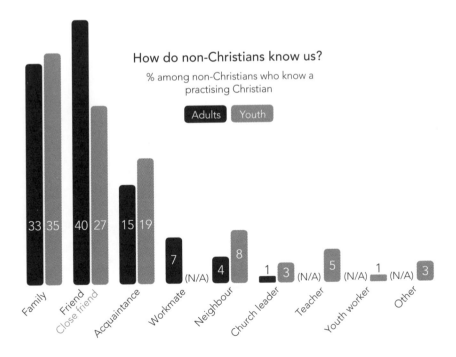

How do non-Christians know us?

% among non-Christians who know a practising Christian

Adults   Youth

	Adults	Youth
Family	33	35
Friend Close friend	40	27
Acquaintance	15	19
Workmate	7	(N/A)
Neighbour	4	8
Church leader	1	3
Teacher	(N/A)	5
Youth worker	(N/A)	1
Other	(N/A)	3

What do people think of us?

The survey results show that non-Christians of all ages like the Christians they know. They're much more likely to describe us as friendly, caring or generous, with very small proportions saying that the Christian they know is homophobic, uptight or hypocritical. And only 6% of young people thought that the Christian they knew was boring.

How non-Christians describe the active Christian they know

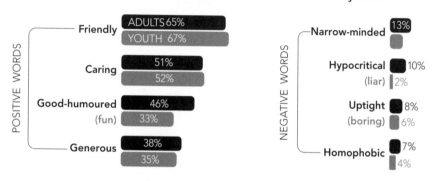

% among English non-Christians
who know an active Christian

Having spoken to a practising Christian they know about their faith in Jesus...

% of those who remained a non-Christian after a conversation

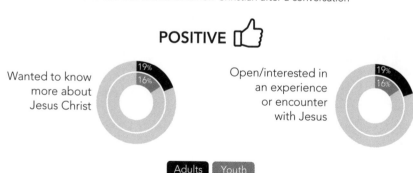

I'm not trying to make it look like a bed of roses but neither do I think it's as bleak a picture as the media would have us believe (and many have believed). Of course there are people who don't know a Christian and a fair number that don't want to know more but let's focus on those that do want to know.

We need to tell the church a different narrative. I see a God who is very much at work and I have chosen to believe him when he said, "I will build my church, and the gates of Hades will not overcome it" or as the King James Version puts it, "the gates of hell shall not prevail against it" (Matthew 16:18).

Jesus wasn't making some inspiration statement like a motivational speaker, nor was he lying like someone wanting to desperately hold onto dwindling followers, or a football manager staring relegation in the face. Fully knowing what was ahead he made that statement based in the revelation of Simon Peter of who Jesus is. We need to make sure all we do in the church is based on that same foundation – nothing more and nothing less.

The Great Commission website

I am sure you will agree the Talking Jesus survey is very encouraging. We need to start telling that different story to our churches. My friend Gav Calver, Director of Mission for the Evangelical Alliance, is committed to doing just that. He and his team have created a fantastic resource called Great Commission (www.greatcommission.co.uk). There is a whole bunch of brilliant resources of all types to help local churches and Christians share the wonderful message of Christianity. They share someone's testimony each week to inspire and remind us that the gospel still works.

The truth is what we are facing now in our culture is not unique to us. I've done enough reading of history and the Bible to know that culture is cyclical. I'm not abdicating our responsibility or suggesting here that we develop a laissez-faire attitude, quite the opposite. I think we need to re-visit some things and some unhelpful historical precedents. Just what did

Jesus mean when he said he would build his church? I'm not sure he quite meant the institution we have become today – not that it's wrong per se but let's not be surprised if there is dissatisfaction with institutional church. The truth is there is dissatisfaction generally with all things institutional, as people feel let down by them.

Now, all that said, I think there are some things we need to consider to help us be more effective and fruitful at reaching out and communicating to people in the here and now. There are some key things we need to consider before I launch into talking more fully about Big Yes, Little Yes, Healthy Maybe, which I would suggest is not some new gimmick but rather new breath into something that is ancient and not new!

These are important parallel principles we need to employ, otherwise we are in danger of looking to a new framework to fix everything. I'm sure you can add to the list!

I list here nine key reasons that we need to address to help our evangelism be more effective:

1. Distortion of the Christian Message

There is a danger in our evangelism that we can "offer" God on the basis of what he can do for people and not on the basis that they need to recognise their need for God's forgiveness, embracing Jesus. Let me add a caveat here: I do believe we can talk about what God does for people outside of the forgiveness he offers, e.g. brings self-worth, but I think we need to present this as a benefit and not the stand-alone reason for accepting Jesus. Accepting Jesus is the doorway to this. Why do I say this? Simply this: over the thirty plus years I have been preaching the gospel I have met too many people who have said to me, "I tried it before and it didn't work." As I chatted further to people I realised they have an unintended distortion of the gospel. An example of this would be when we share our testimony and say to people something along these lines: "When I became a Christian I got peace. If you need peace in your life give your life to God and you will receive his peace as he promises, you will know him close by." The person hearing this reflects that they need peace so they "become" a Christian. We have to be careful we don't unintentionally distort the Christian message.

1. **We shouldn't** become Christians just to get peace.
2. **We don't always** feel that peace, and so the promise is broken.
3. **We don't** always feel God close by and so that promise is also broken.
4. **The result** being it didn't work.

I don't have a problem with talking about what God has done for us and what he can do for others, quite the opposite. I would encourage more and more testimonies about God's greatness and what he can do for us. In fact we are encouraged by David in the Psalms to do this:

Praise the LORD, *my soul; all my inmost being, praise his holy name. Praise the* LORD, *my soul, and forget not all his benefits – who forgives all your sins and heals all your diseases, who redeems your life from the pit and crowns you with love and compassion, who satisfies your desires with good things so that your youth is renewed like the eagle's.* (Psalm 103:1–5)

I often say when teaching Christians about sharing their story that the strength of our testimony is not how bad we've been but rather how amazing God is. This can only be really shown as we tell about the changes that God has made so we clearly need to tell people what God has done for us and what he can, and wants to do for them. The point that I am making here is that we need to make sure we clearly explain what it means to become a Christian i.e. it's about putting God in first place in our life, asking for his forgiveness and making the commitment to turn around the direction of travel in our lives and to follow him; that this is the doorway into all that God has for us and wants to do in us. As I said, I've met too many people who have said to me, "I tried it before but it didn't work." I don't know about you, but I don't want to add to this number.

2. Lack of Good Connection

If you were around Christianity in the 1980s, you may remember the decade of evangelism which was initiated by the Church of England. One of the critiques that came out of that was that Christians didn't have much quality contact with people who weren't Christians. Let me just say at this juncture that I don't blame the decade of evangelism initiative for that!

It's been estimated that between 80 and 85 per cent of people who become Christians do so because of a friend who is a Christian. It's also been estimated that within one year of becoming a Christian most new Christians lose quality contact with their non-Christian friends. It doesn't take a degree in mathematics to realise we have a problem.

In the early nineties we realised that we couldn't simply just preach the gospel and people would become Christians because, the truth is, not many Christians had non-Christian friends. This was even true in the Pentecostal church that I am a part of. Historically we had lived by the motto "come out and be separate" and so we largely relationally disconnected from those around us. Our faith was very church centric in how it was lived out. The gauge of our discipleship was how committed to the church we were. I went to two meetings on a Sunday, prayer meeting Tuesday, home-group Thursday, youth group on Friday, and I was only twelve! Sadly I had no time for relationships with those outside of the church. Even though I had a job with loads of non-Christians I didn't have any time available to meet with them. I had to rush home to get ready for a church event.

In an attempt to redress the balance we were encouraged to "do friendship evangelism" which I don't really have a problem with apart from the relationships became more like evangelistic friendships rather than authentic friendships. I have to say that whilst things are definitely changing there is still a legacy of this in the church. Even now there are some thoughts around that we spend time with people because we must have relationships with those outside the church. The problem with this is we can easily fabricate things.

I remember once in a personal evangelism training session many years ago where I was encouraging people to get some interests. I joked (with serious undertones) that sometimes as Christians we aren't very interesting because we don't have any interests, and that's because our whole life revolves around church – we have few natural connection points. It becomes tricky to really build on anything with this outside the church. The minister came up to me at the end saying that he had felt challenged by what I had said. He told me he was going to do something about it, which was great. I asked him what he going to do and he said, "I am going to join a gym."

"That's great," I said. "Do you like the gym?"

"No, I hate it! I am just joining to make friendships."

So I have a couple of problems with this (and I told him). Firstly, don't get to know people just so you can share your faith with them. Secondly, do something you are actually interested in – it's natural and authentic. I think this is so important.

I remember speaking to a friend of mine who told me he was going to give up spending time with his friend who wasn't a Christian as he just wasn't interested in God. I challenged him by saying you are relationally abusing your friend if you only ever built the relationship bridge so you could get him to become a Christian. Of course I want all my friends to know Christ, why wouldn't you want what's best for someone you care for? Let's invest in quality relationships and pray for quality conversations. Acquaintances happen, friendships are built, and building takes a long time. I'm not giving up on anyone.

3. Bad Witness

A pastor of a church I had been working with some years ago called me. I answered the phone with my customary, "Hello, Mark Greenwood speaking," to which he said, "Oh, hi Mark, just wanted to let you know that you'd be proud of me." I was intrigued, to say the least. He went on to tell me he had just relocated to take on another church and that no sooner had he moved into the manse than he went next door to introduce himself to his new neighbour. I thought to myself, that's a nice thing to do. I have to say from now on it gets a bit less positive. As he continued to tell me about his visit to his neighbour he told me that as soon as he had introduced himself he let his new neighbour (and I quote) "have it". At first I wasn't quite sure what he meant and, in fact, what he had just let his newfound contact have. I asked him to clarify and it was at this point the whole horror show became clear. With great enthusiasm he told me he had let his neighbour have the full gospel, and I mean everything including hell and eternal damnation. After this there was one of those eternal second moments. You know the ones that

I think my pastor friend was disappointed when I broke the dreaded silence with the words, "What on earth have you done, you idiot?"

you experience when you run out of ideas to keep a conversation going with someone who isn't that good at chatting. I think my pastor friend was disappointed when I broke the dreaded silence with the words, "What on earth have you done, you idiot?"

Do your friends know you are a Christian and is that a good thing? You see, the pastor's friends definitely knew he was a Christian but I am just not convinced that was a good thing.

I hadn't long been a Christian when I saw someone wearing one of those

Christian T-shirts that are normally a bit cheesy but this really challenged me. On the back of it were the words, "You are the only Jesus some will ever see." This is really challenging and yet can also (as often these things are) be really inspiring. My pastor friend managed to rebuild with his neighbours, which is great, but sometimes we can affect the way people view God or the church by the way we are. I often pray, "Lord, help me leave a little bit of Jesus wherever I go."

I have a number of mottos which I try to live by. One of them is "making connections – changing perceptions". You see I want my friends to know that I am a Christian, but I want that to be a good thing. I carry a passion to do everything I can to change the perception that people have of Christianity and the church – I think it's one of the biggest challenges we face.

4. Bad Methods

I am going to say something now which I'm not sure I agree with! I'm from Bradford and one day I was walking through the city centre with a friend, heading for that Bradford delicacy, the curry. As we were walking and chatting we walked past a street preacher with a big black Bible who was shouting at people, reminding them they were heading for hell. My friend felt a bit embarrassed and, to be honest, so did I. He expressed this by saying to me, "Listen to that, a terrible witness, he shouldn't be doing that." I asked my friend what he did to tell people about his faith, to which he replied, very honestly, "Nothing really."

I said to my friend, "I think God prefers his way of doing it than your way of not doing it."

My rationale behind this is simple: it's pretty tricky for God to work through us if we aren't doing anything. Is it the best method? No! Should the person learn a better method? Yes! I know people in recent years who have come to faith because they heard a street preacher but how much more effective could we be if we changed our methods.

I strive to be the best speaker that I can be. The message we share is far too precious to get it wrong. I don't have a problem if the gospel is an offence to some (it's biblical) but I don't want the way I share it to be the thing that causes the offence.

I trained in evangelism with a great organisation called OAC Ministries (formerly known as Open Air Campaigners). I am so grateful for what they put into me; it's the bedrock of all I do today. They introduced this verse to me:

> *Assemble the people – men, women and children, and the foreigners residing in your towns – so that they can listen and learn to fear the LORD your God and follow carefully all the words of this law.* (Deuteronomy 31:12)

It's not my purpose here to go into everything they taught about this verse but let me say two things.

Attention: The command was given to assemble. How do you get people to assemble? There has to be an attractiveness i.e. we need to get people's attention. This is true in a geographical sense ("come and see" evangelism) as well as in a conversational sense ("go and tell" evangelism). It's been said about public speaking that if you haven't struck oil in three minutes stop boring! Here's a question about your faith: do those who you connect with know that you are a Christian? And secondly, is that a good thing? I know many people that know a Christian but because of the methods they employ this is not a good thing.

Listen: If I want people to listen to me when I share about my faith it has to be interesting. This means we have to drop the "Christianese". Now I know we all know this but we don't often do it. I can normally tell where a Christian spends most of their time by the words they use. We have our own language! I know someone who uses the word "Hallelujah" as a comma; every sentence they say has an "Amen" or "Praise the Lord" in it. It's like it's a default setting. We need a Christianese detox. Of course if I only spend time in church I don't have much to talk about with people outside of the church.

The other thing which is critical to a person listening to me is that I listen to them. Evangelism is best done in personal conversations and not in personal presentation.

5. Lack of equipping

In the year 2000 Canon J.John had just started doing his Just10 missions and he realised he needed to train more people in evangelism, otherwise people wouldn't bring their plus ones to the Just10 meetings. He said to every Just10 participating church that it was non-negotiable to do his Natural Evangelism course.

In total J.John did thirty-six Just10 missions, the attendance to date of which exceeds one million people. J.John believes we need to equip, train and encourage our flock to become intentional in praying, caring and sharing their faith.

There is often a danger in the church that we talk about the need to do something without actually helping people to do it. For me I am most inspired when I hear *how* I can do something as opposed to hearing I *must* do something.

Time for another personal motto: "inspiration not perspiration". If I am honest, for a fair bit of my Christian life I was challenged to do more – pray more, evangelise more, and so on – and whilst of course I agree with this, I found this cycle taking place: I would hear the challenge and say sorry to God and make a fresh commitment to not do it again; for a while I would do alright then it would all go wrong. You see I don't need someone telling me "You need to" because I already know that. Just to caveat that, I do believe there are times when we need challenge but we can't live there all the time! I love the verse "I can do all things through Christ who strengthens me" (Philippians 4:13 NKJV) but I fear so often we have translated it in practice to be "I must do all things ..."

Many of the evangelism training courses I've seen are not as practical as they need to be. They are often more along the lines of telling us to do it with some tips. They can end up piling more pressure onto Christians to do it as opposed to equipping them to do it.

Why not run J.John's Natural Evangelism training course in your church? HOPE also has a great training course called Talking Jesus and I have a training course called Boot Camp. These are all different in their approach and you could run them over three years.

What about the introvert?

My wife is gifted in conversing with people who aren't Christians. She is very sensitive and wise and knows how to culturally contextualise what she shares.

She is an introvert and so would feel uncomfortable talking at church outreach events like Mums and Tots, but she thoroughly enjoys sitting down and chatting about her faith and exploring tricky questions when there is enough time to do so more deeply, as in Alpha small groups.

When equipping people we need to make sure we don't treat everyone the same. Introverts can be as much evangelists as extroverts but perhaps not in the way we have historically perceived this gifting. Let's make sure we build into our rhythms of evangelism events that benefit from the gifting of all our church members. My desire is that everyone feels equipped so that when opportunities arise they feel confident in those moments and enjoy what they are doing; when people feel pressurised it is rarely fruitful or sustainable.

Apologetics is an excellent way to equip your introverts for topics that will arise during these deeper conversations. I talk about this more fully in Chapter 10.

Whether you are an introvert or not, if you would like to explore evangelism from an introvert perspective, I would recommend as a starter a guest article on the desiringGod.org website by Mike Shumann. He is an adjunct professor and career counsellor at the University of Northwestern St Paul in Minnesota, and serves as a deacon at his church.

Calling all evangelists

Just a word to all the evangelists out there. I firmly believe all evangelists should have equipping dynamic in what they do. Now, clearly, unless you are doing it yourself it's difficult to equip others to do so with example and integrity. Time for another life motto: "Before I am an evangelist and minister I am a Christian." In other words please don't look at how I am doing as a "professional evangelist" (forgive the title) and use that as a gauge of how well I am doing as a personal evangelist. I need to be as intentional on the pavement as I am on the platform!

Training and equipping is so important. Jesus called twelve people to follow him and then spent three years training them. He didn't just tell them to do it; he modelled, he released, he critiqued them. It's not a bad model, is it?

I am honoured to see many people come to Jesus as well as come towards Jesus, but I also get a real joy operating as an equipper. It's not just about the apples on the tree, it's about the trees in the apple!

6. Lack of Motivation

Oh I know all about this. The amount of times I have been inspired and then uninspired as I try to lose weight is impossible to count! Alas, this is not a therapy session so back on topic!

I remember in my younger days when I was an angry young evangelist and couldn't understand why people didn't share their faith. Of course I made the assumption that was the case as I called them out of their apathy! I'm sure many switched off and I don't blame them if they did. Those who were sharing their faith probably did it more; and those who weren't probably carried on not doing it. I'm not sure I accomplished much beyond tiring out those who were already doing it and maybe irritating others.

I have mellowed in my methods even though personally I am more motivated than ever – indeed as I journey myself, at the time of writing I feel less pressured and more privileged than ever that God would use me!

We can be unmotivated for all kinds of reasons and certainly living in the culture we live in now can be demotivating. Have you ever had a bad experience that's put you off doing something again? This is certainly true when it comes to evangelism. We daren't say anything in case we are accused of being arrogant. We fear the accusation of homophobia and we don't need too many negative experiences until we feel deflated and defeated. As time passes, where we were once intentional and active we lose our motivation, often wishing we could get it back. I've certainly prayed for many people who wished they were like they used to be! I think sometimes we put too much pressure on ourselves. I run a course on sharing your faith and my whole ethos is to take the pressure off people.

I am reminded by God's word that "He has committed to us the message of reconciliation" (2 Corinthians 5:19). I did some digging around and discovered the literal translation is more along the lines of "He has put into our hands this ministry of reconciliation." Wow, that puts a different complexion on things and whilst it's about more than just sharing our faith it certainly doesn't exclude it. Have a read of the rest of the passage.

Since, then, we know what it is to fear the Lord, we try to persuade men. What we are is plain to God, and I hope it is also plain to your conscience. We are not trying to commend ourselves to you again, but are giving you an opportunity to take pride in us, so that you can answer those who take pride in what is seen rather than in what is in the heart. If we are "out of our mind," as some say, it is for God; if we are in our right mind, it is for you. For Christ's love compels us, because we are convinced that one died for all, and therefore all died. And he died for all, that those who live should no longer live for themselves but for him who died for them and was raised again. So from now on we regard no one from a worldly point of view. Though we once regarded Christ in this way, we do so no longer. Therefore, if anyone is in Christ, the new creation has come: the old has gone, the new is here! All this is from God, who reconciled us to himself through Christ and gave us the ministry of reconciliation:

that God was reconciling the world to himself in Christ, not counting men's sins against them. And he has committed to us the message of reconciliation. We are therefore Christ's ambassadors, as though God were making his appeal through us. We implore you on Christ's behalf: be reconciled to God. God made him who had no sin to be sin for us, so that in him we might become the righteousness of God. (2 Corinthians 5:11–21)

I would encourage you to meditate on this passage; it's one of those life passages that God has spoken to me through.

7. Lack of Love

Many years ago I was preaching about the thrill of people in a church on a Sunday morning. I was in the flow: "It would be so great if we had a buzz about people. It is true we can like people without loving them but imagine the impact if we liked and loved people, that we had a genuine thrill of people," I said. As I was preaching the aforementioned sermon I experienced something I hadn't before or since. I was talking about the fact that we can't make ourselves love people. As I said this I felt a deep inner conviction and conflict that this wasn't right. In fact I actually stopped mid-sermon and said, "Scrub that from the tape"– kind of shows you how long ago it was I said it! I continued to explain how I didn't feel that sentence was true but I didn't know why. I encouraged the congregation to ignore it. Later that evening as I was driving home in the late hours (a regular occurrence), I was reflecting on why I felt acutely that the phrase "I can't make myself love people" was so wrong. I will never forget the strong sense that God was speaking to me and saying that I could make myself love people by spending time with them. Of course it can have the reverse effect but we won't focus on that. This had such an impact on me.

Let me draw your attention back to the 2 Corinthians 5 passage that I mentioned in the previous section and in particular verses 14 and 15 which say, "For Christ's love compels us, because we are convinced that one died for all, and therefore all died. And he died for all, that those who live should no longer live for themselves but for him who died for them and was raised again." I once heard someone say that the image conveyed here is of a fast-running river, i.e. Christ's love carries us along. I love this.

It has been estimated how far the apostle Paul walked in his efforts to spread the gospel. According to Acts, he took three missionary journeys. The second of these alone amounted to three thousand miles, two thousand of which would have been on foot. The average daily distance of a traveller of that time was about twenty miles, with a Roman inn being located every twenty to twenty-five miles along the road. These inns were unbelievably filthy, immoral, and bug-infested. Paul travelled through snowy mountain passes and spring floods. He walked through areas famous for harbouring robbers and criminals. He braved wild beasts which imperilled every traveller. The travel recorded in Acts 16 alone would have covered 740 miles. That of chapter 15 would be 500 miles. And to think he was walking not for his own health, but for the spiritual well-being of others! You see Paul's outward walking was down to his inward running; he was compelled like a fast-running river with the love of Christ – now that's motivation.

The people I have chosen to spend my life with who aren't Christians are people I am very fond of. As I've spent time with them and got to know them, they have become some of my best friends who are there for me and I for them. There is no shortage of faith conversations – they even invite themselves to events I'm speaking at nearby. This connects with what I was saying a bit earlier in this chapter. Let me encourage you to spend time with people that don't know the Lord.

8. Lack of God's Power

When I first became a Christian there was much preaching about holiness. It seems to not be preached about as much these days for fear of being legalistic. And yet the reality is if I want more of God's power to work in me and through me, that can only happen when the Holy Spirit is able to, and the clue is in his name: he's the Holy Spirit.

Okay, I can only speak for myself and say that there is definitely room for improvement here. I am not as holy as I need to be and I think it's commensurate with how much the Lord works through me. That's not to negate or minimise what I have already written about. I want the Holy Spirit to work because of me and not in spite of me. I love the quote "Work like it all depends on you and pray like it all depends on God". I remind myself, there are no short cuts here; I need to work on my devotional life, therein lies the power. We definitely

I became aware of my lack of equipping about prayer in evangelism.

need to pray more. I confess that I don't totally understand prayer – I mean there's a lot of confusion about it all – but one thing I do know is that God wants me to chat to him about things.

Have you ever had one of those moments in your life when you can't believe you have missed the obvious?

A number of years ago I was looking at all the resources that I had available to churches to help them with their evangelism when suddenly I became aware of my lack of equipping about prayer in evangelism. In one sense I was annoyed and surprised that I had missed this and yet, on reflection, it wasn't just true of my "professional" ministry life; if I am really honest there's a bit of a lack of it in my personal life. That's not because I don't love God or don't feel the need for his power, it's more the case that I am someone whose default setting is to do.

I'm not using this as an excuse, neither am I holding this up as an example; I'm just simply saying this is me. I constantly fight the challenge of "Be still, and know that I am God" (Psalm 46:10) and then get up because there's a lot to do. Whilst sometimes my prayer life can be a bit crazy in terms of rhythm, I do believe that if we pray we see greater impact. There is a lot I don't understand about prayer but what I do know is that it works. Prayer and evangelism, my friend once said, go together like fish and chips – in other words they are best served together. Basically tell God about the world and tell the world about God, it's a great combination. As a result of this I created an event called "How to Prayerfully Invite Your Friends" and it equips and resources people to pray for their friends to come to Christ, helps them to invite their friends along to events (showing the place of events in our evangelism) and then leads to a prayer concert at the end.

So here is a thought: the world's greatest ever teacher, God himself, turned up to our world in Jesus. He called twelve to follow him and he intensely and intentionally equipped them. And then after all that, as he was having a meal with them he said, "Do not leave Jerusalem, but wait for the gift my Father promised, which you have heard me speak about. For John baptised with water, but in a few days you will be baptised with the Holy Spirit" (Acts 1:4,5).

A little bit more chat ensues and then he says, "But you will receive power when the Holy Spirit comes on you; and you will be my witnesses in Jerusalem, and in all Judea and Samaria, and to the ends of the earth" (v. 8).

At the end of Boot Camp, which is a course I run on personal evangelism, I always have time where we ask God for a fresh infilling of his Holy Spirit. I work on the basis that if Jesus felt they needed to get some power after he taught them, I need to do the same! "It's not either this or that but," as my colleague in Elim, Gary Gibbs, can often be heard saying, "it's both and." We need all the areas I have already talked about (probably plus a few more) and the power of the Holy Spirit.

9. Wrong Understanding of Success

We have this strange notion that if we haven't got somebody signed, sealed, delivered and filling in a Gift Aid form we have somehow failed in our evangelism. Okay, maybe not quite that extreme but there is often the pressure of seeing people make a decision that we carry when faith sharing. The crazy thing here is that we are using something that only God can do as a gauge of how well we are, or aren't doing. The sadness is that we can be so preoccupied by the big movement that we don't see the little movement. As I've said before, I have become more convinced that God moves more in the small than he does in the big. This is true in many areas and definitely true in evangelism and people coming to him.

After many years of emotionally and spiritually beating myself up after I preached and didn't see people come to faith, God set me free by reminding me that it was he who convicts people. He reminded me of this verse in the Bible: "When he comes, he will prove the world to be in the wrong about sin and righteousness and judgment" (John 16:8).

If I'm honest I still struggle with it a bit; there is still a feeling out there in the church that we would wheel in the evangelist to throw out the net and bring in the fish.

For a point of clarity I do believe that evangelists can be anointed by God to bring in huge numbers of what I call "Big Yes" commitments but I firmly believe that not all evangelists will do so.

It's interesting that the only definition we see in the Bible about the role of the evangelist is all about "equipping God's people for works of service" (Ephesians 4:12). We are primarily there to equip the Saints for ministry so why do I still use "souls saved" as the gauge of how I am doing? I do believe it's important to gauge impact and outcomes but what are the criteria?

I have to say I am not keen when I hear preachers challenge with the words, "When did you last lead someone to Christ?" I am up for the challenge of when we last shared our faith with someone; that I can do something about. I cannot do anything about whether someone comes to Christ or not. I've learned to not confuse God's part with my part and not forgetting the part of the hearer.

As I was writing this book I felt God remind me again but in a new way (like one of those times when you read a passage that you've read many times only this time it's different) of this passage:

> *Jesus went through all the towns and villages, teaching in their synagogues, proclaiming the good news of the kingdom and healing every disease and sickness. When he saw the crowds, he had compassion on them, because they were harassed and helpless, like sheep without a shepherd. Then he said to his disciples, "The harvest is plentiful but the workers are few. Ask the Lord of the harvest, therefore, to send out workers into his harvest field."* (Matthew 9:35–38)

The part that jumped out at me was "Ask the Lord of the harvest ..." It is God who brings the harvest – he is the Lord of the harvest and I get to bring in the harvest, to collect it not to create it.

Can I encourage you to take on the challenge of "When did you last share your faith with someone?" But don't measure yourself up against someone else's gifting or even God's role i.e. when did you last lead someone to Christ.

#WeCan'tCreateSoulsButWeCanCreateJourney

Journey

After a life of serious crime Ashley Nixon had an encounter with God in prison that would set him on a journey of discovery to real freedom.

I've had the privilege of sharing my testimony of encounter in many different environments, but the more I consider such encounters the more the analogy of the rabbit in the headlights comes to mind. A rabbit crossing a road at night is aware of the possible existence of cars, but the moment the car comes hurtling towards them they freeze: the nearby encounter takes place, its beliefs are further confirmed, but the animal is left wondering how to live in the light of such an encounter. Similarly, the same can happen for those who have faith in Jesus. Yes, the big encounter can be life changing, but it's the day-by-day walk and the continual communion with God that transforms us the most.

Before meeting Jesus I was a true thug, lost in the all-consuming world of drugs. By the age of thirteen I was smoking cannabis, drinking heavily on weekends and occasionally taking ecstasy. By sixteen I'd been expelled from school and prosecuted for burglary, arson, criminal damage and theft. Finally, by the age of nineteen I was heavily involved in drug dealing and gang life to finance my ever-growing habit. Honestly, I don't know what it was that drove me to such anger and destructive tendencies but, as you can imagine, I finally ended up in prison.

In prison I did what I knew best: built my reputation, mixed with others like myself and smuggled drugs into the prison. However, on one occasion I took things a step too far: to build my reputation in a new prison, I decided to borrow tobacco from the loan sharks on my block and refused to pay them back. As you can imagine, this wasn't a wise idea and, following a fight on the landing of my block, the gang placed a price on my head. Now with my life in danger, and the ever-growing fear of entrapment in a life that was rapidly spiralling out of control, I desperately needed help. Thankfully, at this moment another prisoner reached out to me and began to share his faith. He told me that I needed God. Truthfully, this sounded a little crazy but a couple of days later, whilst walking down the corridor on my block, I noticed the sign-up sheet for chapel.

As I walked towards it, a real sense of excitement began to grow within and an internal argument broke out. The moment I tried to walk away, something within began to tug at me to sign-up. Eventually, I gave in to the urge and decided to go to chapel. Once again, as I walked towards the sign-up sheet the sense of excitement grew, and as I wrote my name on the paper a sense of peace hit me that I had never experienced before. Here I was, a broken criminal, receiving exactly what I deserved, yet suddenly feeling a sense of hope and acceptance knowing that there was a way out of the mess that I was in. Truly, I had encountered God in the corridor of prison but, following that, had no idea how to follow through on what I had experienced.

The following weeks passed by. I attended chapel and learnt more about this incredible God that I had encountered. The beating that I was expecting never came. Furthermore, I had a real sense of God's presence, guiding me and protecting me, whilst I served out the rest of my sentence. However, after leaving prison and finding myself surrounded by old temptations, I slowly slipped back into drugs and fighting. Yet I knew that God was real. I held onto the belief that only he could help me. I would go out on weekends, party, take drugs and end up in fights, but then come home, read my Bible and pray. However, it was during this period that the Lord remained faithful to me and continued to work in my life; these were the times when I learnt most about God.

It took a further ten months of study and prayer before I finally came to a revelation of Jesus at church. For me, the Bible was a book and after starting at the beginning it took some time to reach the New Testament. Finally, after giving my life to God in prison, I committed my life to Jesus and then true change began to take place. It's in the valleys, when our backs are against the wall and we're reminded afresh of our inability to serve God or live right before him, that we learn the most. Again, it's the day-by-day reminders of his grace and mercy that remain with us. Thankfully, I write with confidence as a new man, five years clean of drugs, married to an incredible woman, with a theological degree from Bible college. Yet although I've had other such beautiful encounters with God, over my short time as a disciple it's the still small voice and the gentle reminders of his presence that have changed me the most: transformation is a process of being transformed from one degree of glory unto another.

2

Journey – Not Just a Buzz Word

t was a Christmas event; it had gone great with loads of guests present. A man in his early forties headed towards me with a grin on his face. As he got closer he stuck out his hand to greet me and say how much he had enjoyed the event. He then uttered the words I fear most, "You don't remember me, do you?"

To be fair there was a note of familiarity about him but I travel about 30,000 miles per year on the roads of Britain, visiting many churches, but he wasn't to know that! I began to say, "No I don't, I'm sorry, but I meet a lot of people" when I realised I did remember him. We both said it at the same time, "Sunderland – Reason to Believe."

He nodded, "I was the guy ..."

I finished his sentence for him "... who gave me a hard time."

We both chuckled as he said, "Yeah, sorry about that." He told me his sole intention that night was to be annoying.

"To be fair," I said to him, "you managed to do it well." He then told me his story of how about one year ago he had come to Christ and that what had started him was those evenings on the Reason to Believe course. He didn't admit it at the time but they had really challenged his own thought processes. The course didn't convince him of God but it did convince him that his own stand point wasn't thoroughly thought through and that most of what he believed he hadn't really thought about. I was pleased as this is one of the desired outcomes of Reason to Believe. For many, the start of the journey is more about doubting where they are as opposed to believing in God! This story is not uncommon. In fact I would say it's the norm. Sometimes it can happen over an apparently short amount of time but often it's been a number of years and situations that create a journey. Below is further data from the "Talking Jesus" survey.

How do practising Christians describe their journey to faith in Jesus?

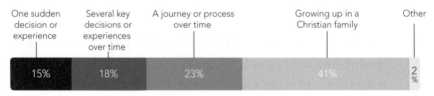

One sudden decision or experience	Several key decisions or experiences over time	A journey or process over time	Growing up in a Christian family	Other
15%	18%	23%	41%	2%

% among adult practising Christians
(Data was not available for young people)

There have been many attempts to quantify it in years, and of course we can only generalise, but it's been estimated that it takes the average person five years to come to faith and that they must hear the gospel approximately twelve times before they will come to faith. I don't know how true this is but what I do know is that "journey" is more than just a buzz word.

The Conversion Journey

I was grabbed by the story of Saul's conversion in Acts 9, and then in Acts 22 where he shares his testimony in front of a crowd, and then again in Acts 26 where he shares it in front of King Agrippa and Festus whilst on trial. Reading these passages together gives some wonderful insights which we miss if they're read in isolation. In terms of shaping my thinking on this process by which people come to faith, this passage has played a leading role.

I've heard so many people share their testimony and start by saying, "I didn't have a Damascus-road experience (referring to Saul's conversion); for me it was much more gradual." The truth is Saul's conversion on the Damascus road wasn't the type of Damascus-road experience we often think it was! Over the next few pages let's consider the story of this incredible event. I mean it was incredible, had it not happened the New Testament would have been a lot shorter! Let's consider these passages – I have inserted them for ease of reference.

Acts 9:1–31

Meanwhile, Saul was still breathing out murderous threats against the Lord's disciples. He went to the high priest and asked him for letters to the synagogues in Damascus, so that if he found any there who belonged to the Way, whether men or women, he might take them as prisoners to Jerusalem. As he neared Damascus on his journey, suddenly a light from heaven flashed around him. He fell to the ground and heard a voice say to him, "Saul, Saul, why do you persecute me?"

"Who are you, Lord?" Saul asked.

"I am Jesus, whom you are persecuting," he replied. "Now get up and go into the city, and you will be told what you must do."

The men travelling with Saul stood there speechless; they heard the sound but did not see anyone. Saul got up from the ground, but when he opened his eyes he could see nothing. So they led him by the hand into Damascus. For three days he was blind, and did not eat or drink anything. In Damascus there was a disciple named Ananias. The Lord called to him in a vision, "Ananias!"

"Yes, Lord," he answered.

The Lord told him, "Go to the house of Judas on Straight Street and ask for a man from Tarsus named Saul, for he is praying. In a vision he has seen a man named Ananias come and place his hands on him to restore his sight."

"Lord," Ananias answered, "I have heard many reports about this man and all the harm he has done to your holy people in Jerusalem. And he has come here with authority from the chief priests to arrest all who call on your name."

But the Lord said to Ananias, "Go! This man is my chosen instrument to proclaim my name to the Gentiles and their kings and to the people of Israel. I will show him how much he must suffer for my name."

Then Ananias went to the house and entered it. Placing his hands on Saul, he said, "Brother Saul, the Lord – Jesus, who appeared to you on the road as you were coming here – has sent me so that you may see again and be filled with the Holy Spirit." Immediately, something like scales fell from Saul's eyes, and he could see again. He got up and was baptised, and after taking some food, he regained his strength.

Saul spent several days with the disciples in Damascus. At once he began to preach in the synagogues that Jesus is the Son of God. All those who heard him were astonished and asked, "Isn't he the man who caused havoc in Jerusalem among those who call on this name? And hasn't he come here to take them as prisoners to the chief priests?" Yet Saul grew more and more powerful and baffled the Jews living in Damascus by proving that Jesus is the Messiah.

After many days had gone by, there was a conspiracy among the Jews to kill him, but Saul learned of their plan. Day and night they kept close watch on the city gates in order to kill him. But his followers took him by night and lowered him in a basket through an opening in the wall.

When he came to Jerusalem, he tried to join the disciples, but they were all afraid of him, not believing that he really was a disciple. But Barnabas took him and brought him to the apostles. He told them how Saul on his journey had seen the Lord and that the Lord had spoken to him, and how in Damascus he had preached fearlessly in the name of Jesus. So Saul stayed with them and moved about freely in Jerusalem, speaking boldly in the name of the Lord. He talked and debated with the Hellenistic Jews, but they tried to kill him. When the believers learned of this, they took him down to Caesarea and sent him off to Tarsus.

Then the church throughout Judea, Galilee and Samaria enjoyed a time of peace and was strengthened. Living in the fear of the Lord and encouraged by the Holy Spirit, it increased in numbers.

A few things to consider ...

1. **Even though** he had a supernatural experience of Jesus it still had to be processed firstly with another person (Ananias) and then in a small group (with the disciples). This tells me a lot about an impressive conversion experience: it needs to be nurtured and one-on-one as well as with a small bunch of people. I am the type of Christian I am today because I wasn't left alone.

2. **Now preaching about Jesus** who he understands more about – talking about his experience. This tells me it's quite important that people start to share their story early on. I know that when I tell my testimony to people it makes me feel a million dollars, which is amazing and faith building as well as letting others know.

3. **Being filled with the Spirit** is really key, as is baptism, and these should definitely be things that we encourage new believers in. Saul had a supernatural life-changing experience of Jesus and was filled with the Holy Spirit and was baptised but, also, he took some food and regained his strength. Sometimes there are some practical things that need to take place when a person comes to faith and these run alongside what we might consider to be spiritual things. Both are important.

Now let's have a look at him sharing his story with a crowd.

Acts 22:1–16

"Brothers and fathers, listen now to my defence."

When they heard him speak to them in Aramaic, they became very quiet. Then Paul said: "I am a Jew, born in Tarsus of Cilicia, but brought up in this city. I studied under Gamaliel and was thoroughly trained in the law of our ancestors. I was just as zealous for God as any of you are today. I persecuted the followers of this Way to their death, arresting both men and women and throwing them into prison, as the high priest and all the Council can themselves testify. I even obtained letters from them to their associates in Damascus, and went there to bring these people as prisoners to Jerusalem to be punished.

"About noon as I came near Damascus, suddenly a bright light from heaven flashed around me. I fell to the ground and heard a voice say to me, 'Saul! Saul! Why do you persecute me?'

"'Who are you, Lord?' I asked.

"'I am Jesus of Nazareth, whom you are persecuting,' he replied. My companions saw the light, but they did not understand the voice of him who was speaking to me.

"'What shall I do, Lord?' I asked.

"'Get up,' the Lord said, 'and go into Damascus. There you will be told all that you have been assigned to do.' My companions led me by the hand into Damascus, because the brilliance of the light had blinded me. A man named Ananias came to see me. He was a devout observer of the law and highly respected by all the Jews living there. He stood beside me and said, 'Brother Saul, receive your sight!' And at that very moment I was able to see him. Then he said: 'The God of our ancestors has chosen you to know his will and to see the Righteous One and to hear words from his mouth. You will be his witness to all people of what you have seen and heard. And now what are you waiting for? Get up, be baptised and wash your sins away, calling on his name.'"

A few things to consider ...

1. Saul was clearly someone who was totally and utterly committed to God. In fact he probably saw Jesus's followers as a bit of a risk to the Jews. Nevertheless Saul had faith and belief in God.

Accompanying my own studies about Paul for this book, I read Tom Wright's brilliant book, *Paul: A Biography*.[1] Tom is writing about what took place in Damascus:

Saul had been absolutely right in his devotion to the one God, but absolutely wrong in his understanding of who that one God was and how his purposes would be fulfilled. He had been absolutely right in his devotion to Israel and of the Torah, but absolutely wrong in his view of Israel's vocation and identity and even in the meaning of the Torah itself. His lifelong loyalty was utterly right, but utterly misdirected. He had a zeal for God, but had not understood what the one God was up to. Everything was now focused on the figure from whom there streamed a blinding light, the figure who now addressed Saul as a master addresses a slave, the figure he recognised as the crucified Jesus of Nazareth. Heaven and earth came together in this figure, and he was commanding Saul to acknowledge this fact and to reorient his entire life accordingly.

So when Christian tradition speaks of the "conversion" of Saul, we need to pause. In our world, as we saw earlier, we normally apply that term to someone who "converts" from one "religion" to another. That was not the point. Not for one second did Saul cease to believe in the One God of Abraham, Isaac, and Jacob. It was just that ... well, what had happened was ... how could he put it? Twenty years or so later he would write of glimpsing "the glory of God in the face of Jesus the messiah." That was one way of putting it. There would be other ways too. This wasn't about "religion," whether in the ancient or the (very different) modern sense. It was about Jesus. About Jesus as the point at which – exactly as the martyr Stephen claimed – heaven and earth were now held together, fused together; it was about Jesus as being, in person, the reality toward which the Temple itself had pointed.

2. Saul needed revelation of who the crucified Jesus was. Until now Jesus was seen as a threat to God where as now Jesus was seen by Saul as the fullness of what he had believed about God. Becoming a Christian is about people recognising who Jesus is and what he has done. For me this is primary. As an aside (allow me, if you will, a slight detour but an amazing one), I love the fact that when Jesus introduced himself to Saul he said, "I am Jesus whom you are persecuting." He didn't say I am Jesus and you are persecuting my followers. That's how much Jesus is touched by the feelings of our infirmities. So Saul's conversion is a recognition of who Jesus is.

3. The previous point we see in Acts 9 but what we don't see there is what Saul says once Jesus has introduced himself. Saul says after this, "What do you want me to do?" You see Saul's conversion was not only a recognition of who Jesus was but it was also a recognition of the fact that Jesus had something for him to do. I felt in recent times that when I call people to follow Jesus it's not just that they are leaving something but that they are connecting with God's purpose. In other words, we aren't just saved *from* we are also saved *for*.

In his book *The Irresistible Revolution*, Shane Claiborne writes,

> Let me remind you that altar calls originated during the fiery revivals of nineteenth-century evangelists like Charles Finney. The reason they gave them was to register new converts for the antislavery movement. They were not simply calling people forward to become new believers; they were calling people forward to join a movement of ordinary radicals. On the altar, belief and action kissed, and extremists for love were born.[2]

Jesus himself called people to leave *for* something not just to leave *from* something.

> *As Jesus walked beside the Sea of Galilee, he saw Simon and his brother Andrew casting a net into the lake, for they were fishermen. "Come, follow me," Jesus said, "and I will send you out to fish for people." At once they left their nets and followed him.* (Mark 1:16–18)

The "at once" shows there was an enthusiasm to lay everything down to follow Christ. I've heard many preacher say that they gave up so much and yes that's true, but it was a real privilege when a Rabbi chose you to follow him, for in asking you do so it was because they saw something of themselves in you which they wanted to develop and release. When Jesus asks us to follow him it's because he sees in us something of himself and that is truly mind-blowing.

As he called those first disciples, he calls us to go and transform his world. I've felt God stir in me in recent times that in my evangelistic preaching I need to emphasise a bit more than I have been doing that God has a plan and purpose for people and that becoming a Christian is about embracing what God has for us.

I realised recently that Ephesians 2:10 is immediately preceded by verses 8 and 9! Now I use the latter, as have many good evangelists before me, to show people that there is no work that they can do that would earn what God has for them. "For it is by grace you have been saved, through faith – and this is not from yourselves, it is the gift of God – not by works, so that no one can boast" (Ephesians 2:8,9). However, verse 10 says, "For we are God's handiwork, created in Christ Jesus to do good works, which God prepared in advance for us to do." You see in our keenness to "save the sinner" and show them there is nothing they can do to get God (which of course is true) we have neglected to tell the whole story, that God has got a whole bunch of stuff that he has called us into which he will use to bring about his kingdom on earth.

It's when we read where Paul tells his testimony in front of Festus and King Agrippa that we glean some further interesting insights.

Acts 26:1–29

Then Agrippa said to Paul, "You have permission to speak for yourself."

So Paul motioned with his hand and began his defence: "King Agrippa, I consider myself fortunate to stand before you today as I make my defence against all the accusations of the Jews, and especially so because you are well acquainted with all the Jewish customs and controversies. Therefore, I beg you to listen to me patiently.

"The Jewish people all know the way I have lived ever since I was a child, from the beginning of my life in my own country, and also in Jerusalem. They have known me for a long time and can testify, if they are willing, that I conformed to the strictest sect of our religion, living as a Pharisee. And now it is because of my hope in what God has promised our ancestors that I am on trial today. This is the promise our twelve tribes are hoping to see fulfilled as they earnestly serve God day and night. King Agrippa, it is because of this hope that these Jews are accusing me. Why should any of you consider it incredible that God raises the dead?

"I too was convinced that I ought to do all that was possible to oppose the name of Jesus of Nazareth. And that is just what I did in Jerusalem. On the authority of the chief priests I put many of the Lord's people in prison, and when they were put to death, I cast my vote against them. Many a time I went from one synagogue to another to have them punished, and I tried to force them to blaspheme. I was so obsessed with persecuting them that I even hunted them down in foreign cities.

"On one of these journeys I was going to Damascus with the authority and commission of the chief priests. About noon, King Agrippa, as I was on the road, I saw a light from heaven, brighter than the sun, blazing around me and my companions. We all fell to the ground, and I heard a voice saying to me in Aramaic, 'Saul, Saul, why do you persecute me? It is hard for you to kick against the goads.'

"Then I asked, 'Who are you, Lord?'

"'I am Jesus, whom you are persecuting,' the Lord replied. 'Now get up and stand on your feet. I have appeared to you to appoint you as a servant and as a witness of what you have seen and will see of me. I will rescue you from your own people and from the Gentiles. I am sending you to them to open their eyes and turn them from darkness to light, and from the power of Satan to God, so that they may receive forgiveness of sins and a place among those who are sanctified by faith in me.'

"So then, King Agrippa, I was not disobedient to the vision from heaven. First to those in Damascus, then to those in Jerusalem and in all Judea, and then to the Gentiles, I preached that they should repent and turn to God and demonstrate their repentance by their deeds. That is why some Jews seized me in the temple courts and tried to kill me. But God has helped me to this very day; so I stand here and testify to small and great alike. I am saying nothing beyond what the prophets and Moses said would happen – that the Messiah would suffer and, as the first to rise from the dead, would bring the message of light to his own people and to the Gentiles."

At this point Festus interrupted Paul's defence. "You are out of your mind, Paul!" he shouted. "Your great learning is driving you insane."

"I am not insane, most excellent Festus," Paul replied. "What I am saying is true and reasonable. The king is familiar with these things, and I can speak freely to him. I am convinced that none of this has escaped his notice, because it was not done in a corner. King Agrippa, do you believe the prophets? I know you do."

Then Agrippa said to Paul, "Do you think that in such a short time you can persuade me to be a Christian?"

Paul replied, "Short time or long – I pray to God that not only you but all who are listening to me today may become what I am, except for these chains."

A few things to consider ...

When Jesus was speaking to Saul on the Damascus road he said to him, "Saul, why do you persecute me, it's impossible to kick against the goads?" A goad was an agriculture tool that was used to steer animals and most often oxen when they were pulling a plough. Fatter at one end and thinner at the other end (similar to a snooker cue), the farmer would prod the ox with the goad to get them moving when they didn't want to, but also to keep them moving in the right direction. The imagery here is that Jesus has been goading Saul to get him moving and to keep him moving in the right direction i.e. towards Christ. What were the goads? We don't know for definite but we know that Saul was present at the stoning of Stephen. There is some thought that a member or members of Saul's family had become Christian and there is strong opinion that Saul would have heard

It was a big moment in a series of moments in his life where Jesus was clearly on his case.

Jesus speaking and seen him perform the miracles he did. Funnily enough, I've heard of many of these spoken about in people's testimonies. I wonder if when Saul shared his story on other occasions whether these occurred in his story. It's clear to me that Saul's conversion on the Damascus road was a significant moment, but rather than it being *the* moment, it was a big moment in a series of moments in his life where Jesus was clearly on his case.

Festus, interrupting Paul's defence, thought he was out of his mind but Paul's response was to say to Festus that he wasn't out of his mind but rather that what he was saying was true and reasonable. We should never feel that what we are sharing is anything other than true and reasonable. King Agrippa's response was very interesting. He said, "Do you think in such a short time you can persuade me to become a Christian?" It seems that King Agrippa's response was much softer, more open to conversation.

Some versions of the Bible translate this as "almost thou persuadest me to be a Christian", however most scholars suggest the more accurate translation is "Do you think in such a short time you can persuade me to become a Christian?" Paul's reply is brilliant, "Short time or long, I pray that you and all those here listening will become as I am, except for these chains."

I remember having a conversation with a friend who said he was giving up with his neighbour. I asked him why this was, to which he replied, "I've tried and tried and told him the gospel but he hasn't become a Christian yet." I did challenge him, telling him that his neighbour isn't a target but he's a person and I shared with him Paul's response.

Much of our personal evangelism and church evangelism tends to be geared more towards the short term but if we can learn anything from Paul's conversion it's that Paul understood more than anyone, that the conversion process is a long-term one that he was committed to praying for.

When Paul said to Agrippa "Short time or long ..." I believe Paul said this because he had a greater understanding of the long-term process than we think. He himself wasn't an "overnight conversion". He already believed in God, in fact this was his upbringing and schooling. What he needed was a revelation of who Jesus was. We live in a world where people don't believe in God and so they are much further back in the process than Paul was.

It's my firm conviction and lived experience that we need to have a long-term view of the journey of commitment. We can spend so much time waiting for the big commitment moment that we don't even see the little steps people take. Let's celebrate and promote whatever steps people take in their discipleship journey – which starts, incidentally, before they come to Christ. We cannot create conversions but we can create conversation. We can't create souls but we can create journey.

The Discipleship Journey

Let me tiptoe into a related subject here that is a separate book but definitely important to connect into this book.

Though this book is not explicitly about discipleship it is implicit in it nevertheless. You can do evangelism without making disciples but you can't make disciples without doing evangelism – like me, you want to get it right!

If you would like to read more about conversion and discipleship I would recommend a brilliant book called *Conversion and Discipleship: You Can't Have One Without the Other.*[3]

> *Then the eleven disciples went to Galilee, to the mountain where Jesus had told them to go. When they saw him, they worshipped him; but some doubted. Then Jesus came to them and said, "All authority in heaven and on earth has been given to me. Therefore go and make disciples of all nations, baptising them in the name of the Father and of the Son and of the Holy Spirit, and teaching them to obey everything I have commanded you. And surely I am with you always, to the very end of the age." (Matthew 28:16–20)*

As an aside, it's worth noting that the more accurate translation should read, "so wherever you go, make disciples of all nations". It carries with it the sense of a daily norm as opposed to a special task!

I believe discipleship starts before someone comes to faith not after. It's a pre-conversion process as much as it's a post-conversion process. Neither evangelism nor discipleship should be based on programme but rather they should be based on process. If we can begin to understand the process behind conversion and discipleship, we can be more fruitful as we interface the two. We have tended to mainly do our discipleship stuff in the context of a collective course. There is nothing wrong with that but discipleship is best done individually. Why? Because not everyone travels at the same pace or from the same place.

Just imagine that I am preaching an evangelistic message in your church. Dave and Sally are guests that day and at very different parts of the journey. Sally has been to Christianity Explored or Alpha but Dave hasn't. As the appeal takes place both Dave and Sally respond to the gospel and put their hands up indicating they both said the prayer. We then invite them and they come along to the discipleship course where they are taught to read the Bible, pray, and be baptised, etc. All this is good but it hasn't dealt with the process of them becoming Christians. You see Dave definitely experienced something and it made him want to give his life over to God. He was impacted by the fact that he could have a new start and have the slate wiped clean. That was very appealing to Dave as he had a slightly chequered past. Sally said the prayer because for her it started to all make sense about the Christian faith as she had been on the course. She realised that she needed to finally embrace God and commit her life to him; this was just the next step for her.

So often we take people through those early stages of nurture and discipleship but don't always do it on the understanding of what is most needed. In the case of Sally she had already done a lot of thinking and asked questions about Jesus and the Bible so her decision was a more informed one, whereas Dave would now have lots of questions about all that. It could seem that one is growing quicker than the other but in truth both were very genuine in the decision they made.

The day I said yes to God, I didn't fully understand the decision I was making. I just saw a load of people who looked like they had something that I wanted and so I committed my life to God. The longer I have been a Christian the more I have understood the significance of the decision I made back then.

A minister friend of mine contacted me expressing concern that someone in his church was still smoking even though he had been a Christian for over twenty years. He asked me for advice. I asked him how long he had been a Christian to which he replied, "Thirty years." I said to him, "You have been a Christian a lot longer than the man you have just talked about to me, but you are still overeating." I have to say he handled it well as he got my point.

We need to be careful that we don't measure everyone's discipleship by the same standard. The danger with discipleship programmes is that we set the same expectations for everyone and that is not the best way of working. It's interesting that in the moments immediately after Saul's conversion he spent time with one person and then with a bigger group – the disciples. I believe that Saul's circumstances were unique to him and whilst there were general things that would relate to him, he also needed the one-on-one. I would like to suggest that this is true for all who come to Christ. It should be about personal pathway not collective course. The fact that the man in the illustration with my minister friend had dropped from smoking fifty cigarettes per day to twenty and had stopped drinking as heavily as he did, showed that he was growing in his faith and in some areas of discipline was arguably further along. We need to make sure that we aren't looking through certain filters when seeing someone else's discipleship and yet remaining blind to our own discipleship deficiency. It's surely about whole-life disciples and, I don't know about you, but I've got a way to go.

Believing, Belonging, Behaving

When I first became a Christian it was very much the case that I believed in Christ, then I belonged to the church, and then my behaviour changed. My observations of the last twenty years or so are that it doesn't quite work like that now. I have seen on many occasions that people have belonged for many years before they believe and even their behaviour has changed. Even as I write this sentence I can see so many faces in my mind of people that I know around the UK in churches that I have preached in who are in this place. I've even known them pray and serve in those churches. It may be that they never make an obvious and external decision but rather they've made a gradual and internal decision.

I remember having a conversation with a minister and his team some fifteen years ago about a man who had started to come to church with his wife who was a Christian, though he himself was an atheist. I was doing what I called back then a "Season of Mission" which basically involved me working over a number of years with a church doing a whole bunch of different level events. I've been doing this for the last twenty years or so.

When I first met the man (he was in the congregation) he was frosty to say the least and it was obvious he wasn't in agreement with most of what I said! Over the years he seemed to soften and ended up going to the house group with his wife. He started to read the Bible between the weekly meetings and he would prepare some questions he could ask based on the passage they were to study the following week. The tone of the questions was very different now, as opposed to when he first asked the question as a means of catching people out. There was now a desire to know answers. He went from saying, "The problem with the Bible …" or "The problem with you Christians is …" to saying, "Well of course as Christians we believe …" or "I know this is tricky but I feel when the Bible says … it is true". He started to come to the church prayer meeting and whilst he didn't pray he was one of the most committed members. He began serving in the church in all kinds of ways. The minister and his team, meanwhile, were still waiting for him to put his hand up after an evangelistic talk and appeal. They didn't think he had become a Christian yet. The interesting thing is if I had asked that team to detail what they would expect of a disciple of Jesus they would probably list all his attributes and also find people in the church who had already put their hand up, as it were, who weren't displaying those attributes.

You could change the person, the church, the city and the year but he/she crops up all over the place – as I said, I can see them now in my mind's eye in some of the churches over the past few years. We have to be careful that we are seeking to produce homogenised conversions and disciples i.e. unless it happens in this way they haven't become a Christian. Let's make sure we don't base our expectation on a model of discipleship that isn't necessarily what Jesus meant when he said, "Wherever you go make disciples."

The following is a contribution from Ed Mackenzie who is an Associate Lecturer at Cliff College, a Discipleship Development Officer in the Methodist Church, and the co-author (with Steven Emery-Wright) of *Networks for Faith Formation: Relational Bonds and the Spiritual Growth of Youth*.[4]

ED MACKENZIE

Big Yes, Little Yes, Healthy Maybe and the Early Church

The Big Yes, Little Yes, Healthy Maybe model is a great help in thinking about evangelism. It recognises that people start at different points as they journey towards Jesus and reminds us that coming to faith takes time.

It's a helpful model, too, because people in today's culture are typically unaware of what Christianity is all about. While they might have positive relationships with Christians, they often don't know what Christians actually believe and why they believe it. They may find the teachings of Christians offensive and wonder why anyone would choose to follow Jesus.

Christians faced similar issues in the early church. As the church grew across the Roman Empire, outsiders were confused about the church and sometimes hostile to new converts. There was a huge gap between the way of life in the culture and the way of Christ in the church.

Within this context, the early church developed an approach to faith formation called *catechesis*. Catechesis was designed to help seekers learn enough about the faith to make a decision for or against it. It helped them to learn how Christians worshipped, what Christians believed, and how they were called to live.

Catechesis formed disciples who had truly counted the cost of discipleship, converts who knew what they signed up for when they confessed Jesus as Lord. Catechesis was a kind of training for discipleship, a way to help followers "fight the good fight of faith" (1 Timothy 6:12).

As we invite people to the way of Jesus today, we can learn from the historical practice of catechesis. It can prompt us to think about how best to help seekers learn the way of Jesus and how to equip converts to begin to walk in it.

Catechesis helps seekers know what it means to worship God.
Catechesis has often helped seekers and disciples grow in their worship of God through engaging with the Lord's Prayer, the model prayer Jesus gave to his disciples (Matthew 6:9–11). But worship is also about keeping God as first in our lives, loving God with our whole beings (Mark 12:29–30) and turning away from the idols that distract us.

In today's society, evangelism can help seekers understand how the call to worship turns us from a gospel of self to the gospel of our Saviour. It can invite seekers to take part in the worship of the church while showing how the gospel dethrones the idols of our culture such as consumerism, relativism and the worship of success.

Catechesis helps seekers learn what Christians believe. In the early church, converts had often been shaped by a range of non-Christian teachings and philosophies and so needed to learn what was different about trusting Jesus. In teaching the faith to religious seekers, Christians often used the Apostle's Creed as a guide. The Creed offered a short-hand summary of key Christian beliefs as well as a way into the riches of Scripture.

Today, too, people are shaped by beliefs and a worldview very different to the Christian faith, and so helping people grow in the way of Christ means teaching them what Christians believe and why they believe it. Courses like Alpha and Christianity Explored offer useful models in this, but there are a range of new and creative ways to help converts as well as seasoned disciples grow in their knowledge of God's truth.

Catechesis helps seekers learn how to live the way of Jesus. Christians in the early church helped seekers and converts grow in faith, hope and love, and often used the Ten Commandments (interpreted in the light of Christ) as a key framework for such teaching. Those exploring the faith were helped to understand the way of Jesus and were taught ways to strip off the old self and put on the new (Colossians 3:9–10).

In a culture where living as a Christian is deeply countercultural, churches need to intentionally instruct seekers and equip converts in the way of Christ. Coming to Jesus involves nothing less than a complete overhaul of one's life! Disciples are those who live and die for their Lord (Romans 14:7–9), those who bear the Spirit's fruit and turn away from sin (Galatians 5:16–26). The church is called to reflect the life of the kingdom, teaching the way of Jesus and giving glory to the Father by lighting up the world (Matthew 5:14–16).

While *catechesis* may be an ancient term, the process of faith formation it involves is helpful to recall as we evangelise and seek converts today. Part of their journey has to be learning the way of Christ sufficiently to say the "big yes" to Jesus. And when they've said that yes, the church is called to help them – and to help us all – to grow more deeply into God's love and grace.[5]

The need to journey with people isn't a recently created buzz word but rather an ancient biblical principle which deserves to be re-discovered and should never have been lost.

When I first became a Christian the measure of commitment was church-centric. We need to have a different approach and gauge in the culture we live in. I say all this as one who totally believes in the local church, but is the only valid expression of local church on Sunday morning at 10:30 a.m. or at a midweek small group? Just to clarify, I'm not saying that these are outdated – not at all – I'm simply saying that we are in danger of thinking that people don't want to belong just because they don't come to a traditional model of church.

As I write this book yet more high street brands are having to change the way they work as more and more people buy online. Before I came into full-time evangelism in 1988 I was a butcher. I worked in a beautiful Victorian market that had about twenty butchers' stalls, twenty fishmongers' stalls, and fruit and veg stalls, plus a selection of cooked-meat shops and delicatessens. There was even a shop dedicated to selling that Yorkshire delicacy, pie and peas.

I remember my boss Donald expressing his concern about the big supermarkets and out-of-town retail outlets killing the independent traders. Fast forward thirty years to today and now the online traders are killing many of the shops that took trade from the city centres. Many of these victims are stores that either refused to change or simply lived in denial of the change in buying culture. Not only is this the case with buying trends but also the development of technology. Woolworths, Blockbusters, Marks and Spencer, British Home Store, Debenhams, John Lewis to name but a few are all either no longer trading or facing major changes as to how they stay alive let alone thrive. Could we add church to this list? I hope not. I hope we are big enough to move. Some of my concerns are that we

We hold onto cultural models from the past as though they are biblical models.

hold onto cultural models from the past as though they are biblical models. The truth is they were models that culturally worked enabling biblical principles to be carried out in a relevant way. We need to understand the times and know what Israel should do.

So, what is the most effective way to make disciples in today's culture? Let's be honest enough and bold enough to change where we need to change however uncomfortable it makes us feel.

I love Allan Hirsch's book *Forgotten Ways* which, in a nutshell, encourages us to look back and look deeper to rediscover some true biblical understanding of what it means to be a community of disciples on mission. He says, "It isn't that reading into our past is not part of the solution. It is. The issue is simply that we generally don't go back far enough, or rather, that we don't delve deep enough for our answers."[6]

I found the book a real encouragement and would definitely recommend a read. The interesting thing is that this isn't a new book but it certainly speaks right into the heart of where we are today. So often we can see what we have in today's church as a biblical model and yet if we go back to the early church we get a different story. There is nothing wrong with the model of church today per se but we have to be careful that we haven't made it an idol, i.e. this is the only way that is right. The better way is to go back to God's original plan for church and ask how we can best translate that into the culture that we are in, enabling us to best make disciples today.

The Journey Towards and Through Change

Question: How many therapists does it take to change a light bulb?

Answer: None, the light bulb has to really want to change.

My friend Duncan Logan is a cognitive behavioural therapist and a really good friend (no link!). He is also passionate about community and reaching his friends who aren't Christians. One day I was telling him about this book and what I felt God was revealing to me about the process by which people come to faith. I expressed to him that there was a human dynamic in the way people are willing to come to faith as well as a spiritual dynamic, neither of which should be ignored. He shared some very helpful insights about how people journey towards and through change which I and he observed were true of those we know and see who are coming to Christ. He writes:

DUNCAN LOGAN

Have you ever tried to get a friend to stop smoking when they are not ready? It is impossible because people only change when they are good and ready. This applies to becoming a Christian and the cycle of change that needs to take place before making a decision to follow Jesus.

The one thing I know as a therapist is change is not easy. What has helped me understand it more is "The Cycle of Change" by Prochaska and DiClemente. It recognises that people go through various stages when it comes to making changes, and most significantly have to be ready to do so. There are six key stages they outline that help us through the process of change:

Pre-contemplation

The first stage is where a person has no intention of changing behaviour, or they may be unaware that a problem exists. If this is the case, you can only build relationships with them and give information that may lead them to contemplate change.

When my wife and I first met Steven and Gail at our school summer fate, they were not even contemplating what life was all about never mind God – they had a good life. Steven, like me, was a keen cyclist so we started cycling together twice a week, while Jackie got to know Gail. We quickly became good friends sharing a heart for community and social events. It was while cycling together that Steven and I started to get to know each other. We would talk about life and family; we laughed together and just had a great time.

I could not talk about my life without talking about my faith, my love for Jesus and the importance of our church family. The God conversations lasted 5–10 minutes at a time but something began to shift in Steven. He started asking questions about my faith, he seemed to listen more intently, and talk about his experience of faith. He was beginning to think about the things we discussed – he was shifting into the contemplation stage.

Contemplation

It is at this stage where people recognise there may be a problem that exists but are not ready to commit to change. They may feel they aren't able to make the change. At this point you help them see the benefits of change and believe they can do it.

On someone's journey to faith this would be inviting them to less threatening events such as home group socials. With Steven and Gail we invited them to spend time with us as a family. We invited them to the children's church Christmas party and we introduced them to our Christian friends. When our daughter was Mary in the church nativity, we asked them if they wanted to come. They said they would love to see Abigail in the play. I believe this was not the only reason, they also wanted to check out church. We pray for them constantly to move into the next stage in the cycle – the preparation stage. In the meantime we will continue enjoying doing life together.

Preparation

In this stage a person is intent on taking action and begins to make the necessary preparations for this. In faith this could be attending church events or courses run for people exploring faith. They ask, "What do I have to do in order to make change possible?"

Action

This is the crunch point. They know they need to make the change, they see the benefits of change, they have even made preparations to make the change, but now they have to take action and make the change.

When someone comes to see me for therapy they will most likely be at least in the contemplation stage, or more likely the preparation stage. This is because they have got to the point where they have decided to seek help as they recognise there is a problem. Together we will formulate the problem which involves exploring how it developed, the impact on their lives, and what keeps it going. If done well it makes sense to the client and will help create a treatment plan for the next phase of therapy. This incorporates what change looks like and what they need to do to facilitate meaningful change. The client at this point has to decide whether they are ready to make the changes and accept what that might mean. As difficult as their life is at present there is something familiar and comfortable in what they know, and change often comes at a cost.

Maintenance

This stage follows the decision to take action. The client starts changing old behaviours and replaces them with new behaviours. Initially I see my clients weekly when they need more support while making difficult changes and overcoming obstacles. As they begin to make more consistent changes, we will leave it longer between sessions. Eventually, as we prepare for discharge, we discuss good support networks and what they need to continue to put into practice to maintain the gains they have made.

In someone's journey to faith they have accepted Jesus. They are journeying from their old life to the new which they need help navigating. When Steven and Gail make that decision, they will need discipling through the maintaining stage as their faith takes route. We will work through blips and challenges which gradually they can work through themselves. Most importantly we prepare them for the next phase which is relapse: a falling back into old patterns that created and maintained the original problems.

Relapse

Preparing clients for relapse is extremely important because it is a normal part of making difficult changes. The pull of the old thinking and behaviour habits can at times be very strong, especially if we are going through difficult life events. It is important to prepare people for relapse to help them manage it when it comes. The great thing about the cycle is you can always start again. There is always the possibility of people who make a decision to fall back into the patterns of the world. To be drawn to the life they had before. If you have built a solid friendship you will always be there to begin the cycle with them again.[7]

Do not conform to the pattern of this world, but be transformed by the renewing of your mind. Then you will be able to test and approve what God's will is – his good, pleasing and perfect will. (Romans 12:2)

The Bible places a lot of emphasis on the mind; no surprise it's a battle ground and I believe we need to allow for that process in the journey of faith.

Big Yes, Little Yes, Healthy Maybe

Big Yes, Little Yes, Healthy Maybe is not a gimmick, a manipulation or a formulaic approach, but rather it's recognition of the phases that most people go through when coming to faith as helpfully explained by my friend Duncan previously.

As we conclude this chapter I want to briefly set out my intentions for the next three.

- I will define BYLYHM so that if you feel you want to start to use them in your evangelism then you do so with understanding. I think this is important as already I am preaching in churches that have started to use them with non-Christians present. The agreed definitions will minimise any confusion.

- I will begin to dig a bit deeper into the definitions and how they work out in a person's life.

- I will give examples I have come across and been involved with.

#WeCan'tCreateSoulsButWeCanCreateJourney

Journey

Jason Heron had no church background but after an encounter with God which troubled him, in a church service where he had gone to cause trouble, a journey of discovery started that would radically change his life forever.

One Sunday evening I was invited to a church service. My dad and brother-in-law had attended the church over the past few days and both had made a decision to become Christians. The main reason I accepted the invitation was to cause trouble in the meeting. I wanted to get back at my dad as at this time our relationship was not at its best. I arrived at church with four of my friends. The service was full and the only seats available were on the back row.

Apart from weddings and funerals this was the first time I'd attended church. The experience was something new as the songs were different to what I expected and the people in the meeting looked really happy to be there. After the singing had finished we were invited to be seated. I was busy looking for my dad. As I said, my plan was to disturb the meeting, which I wanted to do and then leave just so he could be embarrassed.

I was just about ready to do that when a man was introduced and he came to the stage. He began to talk about God and Jesus and, as he did, a weird feeling started inside me. It was strange because I wasn't really paying attention – I didn't understand what he said – but when he began to talk about Jesus, that's when the feeling started. I became very emotional and very confused; I was at the point of tears and I didn't know why.

As the speaker continued to talk I heard him say that this Jesus could give real meaning to life as well as his peace and purpose. I am sure he said lots more but these were the words that I could not shake off. At that moment it was as though he was speaking to me about my life. I had most things that were said to bring happiness and peace. I had money, new cars, great holidays, friends and a loving family, and yet I was still not fulfilled – it all left me feeling lonely and insecure. Was it me thinking this or someone else?

Then the speaker continued with his sermon and when he got to the end he asked if there was anyone who would like to give their life to Jesus. Instantly my hand was raised in the air and at that moment I left my seat to walk to the front of the church. All I can remember was saying to myself, or to God, that if he was real, not to let me leave the church the same. It was then I experienced a weight suddenly lifting from me and I knew that God was real. As I returned to my seat I invited my friends to give their lives to Jesus too. From that night my life was never the same again.

So what was the process of my conversion? I wasn't a churchgoer. I was from a Romany Gypsy family. The only thing I can remember in my family that expressed any vague interest in God was the series *Jesus of Nazareth* which my dad watched over several weeks on television. As I watched the film and saw people rejecting Jesus, I thought to myself that if I was there at the time I would have believed in him, although I'm not really sure why I thought this. My only other connection was that I was given a Gideon's New Testament Bible at school and I would say the Lord's Prayer occasionally, but that was it.

After a night out clubbing I arrived back at my mobile home and was just leaving my bathroom when a voice in my head told me that if I looked in the mirror I would see the devil. I felt the real presence of evil in the room. The fear that gripped my life at that moment caused me to reach for the Gideon's Bible I had still kept with me from school. As I read it the presence left me and a different presence entered. This was just a few weeks before I was invited to the church where I wanted to cause trouble.

I had left school at fifteen with no education (my parents didn't value it). I had no knowledge about God – I didn't even know God and Jesus were the same – and yet I was converted and became a fully committed follower of Jesus. I suppose I said a big yes to God or Jesus but had little understanding of them, or anything else about Christianity to be honest.

After weeks had passed I was encouraged to read the Bible and attend church. You see I had no idea how this all fitted together. I knew nothing about being born again or salvation or repentance and sin. These only became clearer as I continued on the journey. All I know is that something had happened to me on the night that I had intended to show my dad up. I didn't fully appreciate what had happened but I knew something had.

Some suggest that we need to fully understand with our mind the basics of what it means to become a Christian and connect with God. It can work like that for some but it didn't for me. I made the decision and then began to learn and understand. Some people go on a journey to faith on something like an Alpha course but in my case I said a Big Yes to faith then went on an introduction to the Christian faith; I would say lots of Little Yes steps.

The first two months of my journey were amazing; it was as though I would hear God speak to me on a daily basis and he would tell me things and show me what to do. My life choices would change because of the love and freedom I was experiencing – I could not keep it to myself. Then, through the people in the local church who had more understanding, I continued to grow as they helped me on my journey.

It is twenty-eight years on from that day and my journey of learning still continues as I understand more about the vast nature and love of God, as well as his unfolding purpose for my life. It is a day I can't forget. I was not looking for God but he was looking for me.

The Big Yes

THE BIG YES: saying a heartfelt "yes" to God; becoming a Christian.

Have you ever been confronted by a double-glazing salesperson? "You pay for your upstairs windows and we will give you your downstairs windows completely free of charge." Quite apart from the fact I'm not sure I believe the "free of charge" bit, the major problem I have with this sort of marketing is that it's nearly always "sign now or you miss it". Whenever I've asked for some information to take away to consider and then decide, this is nearly always never an option. We have to be careful that we don't do a "now or never" style approach in our evangelism.

I remember when I first started out in evangelistic preaching and was probably a bit over-passionate; by that I mean I came across a bit angry. I would say things which looking back now I am a bit embarrassed about. I remember coming to the end of my talk and inviting people to come to Christ. I would say, "If you are not saying 'yes' to God then you are saying 'no'." It was basically the "if you were to be run down by a bus having not said yes to Christ ..." style of approach. This was normally the peak of a gospel rant!

The problem was then, and is now, just because someone isn't saying "yes" to God, it doesn't mean they are saying "no". If, however, I only offer them a "yes" or "no", they will probably say "no" because they cannot fully say "yes". This doesn't mean we shouldn't offer the Big Yes moment; in fact I believe we should do it more as we seem to have shifted away from this. There are many people who are ready to

"If you are not saying 'yes' to God then you are saying 'no'."

respond in this way. What it does mean is that we need to make sure that we offer people a way to respond that is both decision and journey focused.

I want to put a marker down here just in case you misunderstand. I believe 100 per cent in giving people an opportunity to say the Big Yes to God. It's an important part of my evangelistic ministry and in truth we don't see it done enough. My fellow evangelist friends and I see many people responding to the gospel and whilst there are recommitments in amongst those, there are many for whom it is the first time. We have to remember when people hear the gospel some will have already been on a journey and aren't far away from responding. If we aren't careful we can be so focused on the process that we forget the decision. Conversely we can be so focused on the decision that we forget the process. For me it's about synergising both thinking and encounter. There are people who are encounter conversions i.e. they have a very real spiritual experience of God, and there are some who are thinking conversions i.e. they need a long time to process and then they become Christians (more about that in the next chapter). Now that's not to say that those who encounter don't think, they do but most of their thinking is post that big moment. I think one of the things I love about the Alpha course is that it facilitates the thinking and the encounter.

I believe people must be given an opportunity to say the Big Yes to God and what I want to do here in this section is to look at what that means and how we can do it better. It was dissatisfaction with not doing it well that set me on a journey years ago, of which this book is the culmination of what I have processed so far.

Don't Decide For Them

So often we have amazing times sharing our faith and then we don't give people an opportunity to become a Christian – it's almost like we have decided for them as opposed to giving the opportunity to them. I totally understand we don't want to pressurise people coming to faith in God. We are fearful of the giving the Big Yes for a number of reasons. I think there is some sense of, "What if they don't want it?" The fear of rejection plays a part here but again they might not be ready to commit and that's okay. Sometimes in our evangelism we can end up at both extremes where we are guilty of being too forceful or too frightened to lead a person to Christ. I have come up with a solution to the tension: I ask them!

I was once sharing with a friend of mine over coffee how I felt God was challenging me in my faith-sharing. I wanted to have the same level of confidence in my personal evangelism as I had in my professional evangelism. You see I had no problem giving people an opportunity to receive Christ from a platform but I didn't have it in a one-on-one context. Now granted it is different when speaking to many as you aren't eyeballing them, and also you are addressing a broad range of places on the journey but, all that said, I took the challenge from God.

We left the coffee shop in Loughborough where we had enjoyed a latte and the chat. As we walked back to church we were approached by a young man working for a charity collecting organisation. As we chatted he asked us what we were doing. Long story short, as we told him we were ministers the conversation turned to us sharing the gospel with him and, well, as you can imagine, I had that Holy Spirit nudging thing, "Go on, then, don't just talk about it over a latte, do it." Well you will be pleased to know that I didn't bottle it; I asked him and he said yes, so we led him to the Lord right there on the streets. We were buzzing but we stayed calm until we got around the corner and then there may have been a fist pump and a "thank you, Lord".

There are times when it is right to just go for the Big Yes and we certainly need to be open to the Holy Spirit in this. There are some speakers who have a gift of reaping a harvest and it's crucial we plan for this.

The stories at the beginning of each chapter show that in the main it tends to be a journey for most people but for many of them there are critical moments of decision and some of my friends who are evangelists are used by God to bring people to that critical moment. I am yet to find someone who has gone from atheist to believer without some kind of journey, though I am sure there will be some out there. I believe that making evangelistic appeals for people to come to Christ, whether in a small venue or large scale event is still fruitful today. But let's remember that for those who say the Big Yes in these moments there is just as much of a process going on "post decision" and it should not surprise us if people have doubts or even don't fully believe or understand everything they heard. When I gave my life to Christ I didn't fully understand what I was doing; what I did know is I had to respond. The longer I've been a Christian the more I understand about the significance of the moment. The way people come to Christ tends to be through a process peppered with crises i.e. over a long journey people have key moments where they make decisions. We limp along in our evangelism if we don't allow and facilitate both of these.

Post-decision Journey

We have to make sure that when people say the Big Yes to God that we don't treat it in a generic way. There is a danger of having a "right, they are in" mentality, i.e. they are now a Christian. Now it's not my purpose here to debate that but rather to help that.

Often when people respond to Christ they do so as they feel something. Whenever I have nurtured new believers there is a realisation that they responded to a specific part of the message, for example God's love, but didn't necessarily relate to or understand the other stuff, for example repentance. Similarly, people can have doubts about God's love for them and we are speaking about praying and reading the Bible (all of which we should speak about, by the way) but this isn't dealing with the personal need. Let's maybe give them some things about God's love for them to read from the Bible and that they can pray over their lives daily. Similarly, if an individual is struggling with assurance we need to work with them on that as opposed to something more general.

I remember when I was young and very new to the faith I would have doubts and struggles. Those more experienced people simply told me it was the devil so rebuke him. Well I would go into my room and shout at him and send him back to the pits of hell but, if I am really honest, no amount of verbally claiming the victory really worked. I needed to be able to externalise my doubts, yes to God, but actually also to others, rather than pretending everything was alright whilst practising my daily verbal sparring match with the devil and never really progressing.

When people come to faith over a long period of time and therefore have lots of opportunities to express their doubts with other people, something amazing happens:

> **1. They externalise their doubts.** Back in the day we would call this "bringing it into the light". I believe this as it helps stop the doubts nibbling away in our minds.

> **2. They discover** that people who have been Christians longer than they have, also have spoken of the same doubts (that is if they are honest), but are still following God.

Doubts externalised as opposed to doubts internalised are really important. This doesn't mean that the doubts aren't there but what it does mean is they can have less of a grip.

Decisions, Decisions, Decisions!

I lease a car; it makes absolute sense for me. It works out best financially as I save money and also can plan my car spending. Not only that but the car's reliable, meaning that I get to the event I am speaking at! Every two years I am approached by the dealership offering a new car at the same price. I know it's the right thing but I have to go through the same process every time. I finally decide: I'm going to do it. I sign on the dotted line and then have a mild panic attack! What have I done?

Most people go through accepting rejecting, accepting rejecting many times before they finally accept. Even when they finally accept they can still have doubts. This isn't just true of becoming a Christian, it's perfectly normal. This is true of normal life and any change we go through as we learned earlier in Chapter 2 with my friend Duncan.

Saying "yes", then, doesn't mean they are fully embracing or even understanding, they are simply responding to the nudge of the Holy Spirit. The day I said yes to God I didn't fully understand the significance of what I was doing. The longer I have been following Christ the more I understand the significance of that decision back in June 1982.

What I did have, however, is the opportunity to work it through and work it out as I benefited from good nurture and discipleship.

Don't be worried if after a Big Yes they end up having some doubts. As I write, it's fifteen months since my most recent decision to lease another car (four so far) and I'm still asking myself if I've made the right decision.

What about Those Who Fall Away?

I have tried many diets: Slimming World, Weight Watchers, calorie counting and basic starvation. I often did really well, even getting to target weight, but the real battle often kicks in when you try to maintain!

I have done some amazing exercise. At one point I was running two ten-kilometre runs each week as well as cycling to my office twice a week, which was about a twenty-two mile round trip. I threw in a couple of shorter runs for good measure. It was all going really well and then ... ! What was the then? Well, it was more like three thens. In the period of about twelve months a car ran over my foot as a result of which I sustained a crush injury. Then just as I started to feel I could run again I did my hamstring in preaching (I know, don't ask!), then just as that was getting to the stage where I could go running again I cracked a rib fixing the downstairs loo at home, and then just as that was healed and I could start running again I got a severe chest infection that lasted for about three months. It's been a while since I have been running!

I'd made the big decision to lose weight and get fit and I set myself a goal but then it was all about the daily discipline of sticking with the decision. There were times where I did well and times that I didn't and where I felt like giving it up.

Ever since I have been a Christian I have responded to challenges in sermons with great enthusiasm and I have done really well for a season but then, as my friend Duncan the therapist would say, the "relapse stage" kicks in. So if this is true for those of us who have been Christians for a long time, why wouldn't it be true for those early on in the faith?

I have a friend and I think he must hold the record for the quickest falling away from God ever. Before you think I am making light of it, I'm not; he's full on with God now and we have both chuckled over his story. He became a Christian on Friday evening and then woke up on Saturday morning wondering what on earth he had done. He actually said to God, "I want to take that back" (the decision to follow Christ that he made the night before). I would love a theological debate on that one!

I am under no illusion that however long or quick it takes someone to come to faith in Christ and however intense or brilliant our discipleship is, that it is not a guarantee that all will stick with Christ. I don't hold to the view that people who have a genuine encounter with Jesus will always stick with him.

I sometimes ask the question of how many disciples abandoned Jesus. Most people answer, "One – Judas." In truth all of the disciples abandoned Jesus until he appeared to them, which we can read about in the Great Commission. I mean, as encounters go, spending three years with Jesus pretty well all day every day is a great encounter in my book. Even when Jesus stood amongst them and they all bowed down in worship there are three very revealing words – "but some doubted" (Matthew 28:17). Spending all that time with Jesus was all about encounter and discipleship but still they fell away and, in some cases (Simon Peter for example), completely denied Jesus publicly and Judas, to the best of our knowledge, never returned to Christ. Knowing that they would abandon him did not stop Jesus calling them to drop everything and follow him.

We shouldn't stop calling for a Big Yes knowing that some will fall away. If my theology serves me right, God knew that Adam and Eve would sin but he still made them. Jesus knew that the disciples would abandon him and yet he still called them to follow him. Jesus knew that Judas would betray him for thirty pieces of silver and yet he still trusted him with the purse! The Parable of the Sower teaches us some useful things about the seed and the soil and how it grows or doesn't grow. I have a few thoughts on that but may need to write a blog as opposed to talk about it here.

Can I be so bold as to call for a renewed desire and practice of giving people an opportunity to follow Christ, coupled with an understanding of the conversion process?

#WeCan'tCreateSoulsButWeCanCreateJourney

Journey

Unaware that one of her best friends was praying daily for her, Joanna lived her life with no belief in God. But as her friend journeyed with her for twelve years, she would eventually come to know the God of her family for herself.

I grew up in the beautiful country of Northern Ireland on a farm, surrounded by my wonderful family and a lot of cattle.

I was aware from an early age that my family had a faith and it was always an active part of our lives. But fast forward a few years and my parents' faith took a leap, a huge one. We were moving, from the place I had always known as home, to a new home and a new country. We packed our bags, filled up the car with our belongings and we said our tear-filled goodbyes. Hours later we boarded the ferry and made our way across the channel, to our new home, with no idea what was in store. My parents felt called to study theology full time and this was the next step on their faith journey. We lived onsite with all the other students and very quickly the community we were now a part of became family. I remember how nervous, scared and worried I was about starting a new school, making friends and settling in to this very new, very different way of life. Here was where I was to meet some of my closest friends.

On the first Sunday after we arrived, we visited the local church. That's where I met my new friend: she was thirteen, I was twelve; she had brown hair, I had blonde. We clicked straight away, mostly over our mutual love of Taylor Swift. We began to do everything together, and before long we were the best of friends. We shared and journeyed through the highs and lows of growing up but always stuck together. There was one main difference though; she followed Jesus and despite my upbringing I was unsure what I believed. I knew the Bible verses, the stories and I had heard what Jesus had done on the cross but it never landed, not fully. I had many unanswered questions – questions around my worth that led me to seek my affirmation from the wrong places; questions around suffering, how can such a good God allow such bad things to happen, not just to people across the world but to me. When I was a child I was diagnosed with diabetes, and as a result it changed the way I lived my life. I had operations to try and change the outcome but eventually I had to accept that this would become a daily part of my life. I needed an outlet for my questions and it led me to point them in the direction of a God I didn't believe in. I couldn't equate that a good God would allow me to suffer from a disease that affected my whole life and so I wrote God off from an early age.

As the years went on I wanted less and less to do with Christianity. I was making a life for myself, I was in a long-term relationship, focusing on progressing in my career, I enjoyed going out every weekend with my friends and enjoying nice holidays. Frankly I didn't see the need to have God in my life. My life was made, from the outside looking in at least. However, the reality was very different. I was learning fast that there was a hole in my life that couldn't be filled, no matter how hard I tried to fill it with relationships, success, money.

Despite my disinterest in having a relationship with God, my relationship with my friend always remained. She was such an amazing friend who I could always rely on and, no matter what, she always showed me love and support. She understood my questions and doubts, and always wanted to journey with me through them. It would have been so easy for her to give me a theological answer to all my questions, but instead she would often acknowledge that she didn't have all the answers or that in fact she had struggled with the same questions I had. It made me understand and recognise that God is big enough to handle my questions, my doubts and my unbelief.

Little did I know that she was praying for me, daily, that I would come to know Jesus. We would often have conversations about faith: I would ask the questions and she would answer, sometimes with another question but she was consistent with her faith, and that stood out. Her dependency on God, her passion for the gospel and her commitment to living out her faith was tangible.

She didn't see evangelism, sharing her faith, as a moment or one encounter but as a journey, in fact a journey that lasted twelve years. That's how long, from the time we met, it took me to say yes to Jesus, to say I'm all in!

She is still one of my best friends to this date but instead of me being the one with all of the questions, we both explore our questions around faith together. We pray for each other. Who would have thought? I know who ... God knew all along and I'm so thankful that he placed this friend in my life.

So whether you have been journeying with someone for a few weeks or a few years, know that God is using you, whether you realise it or not, in their story. Don't be put off by their questions and unbelief. Just keep trusting that God can use your life to reflect him. I heard someone once say that "you only need to reach one Samaritan woman to get a whole village". It took years for me to come to a place where I finally accepted Jesus, so don't give up on those you are praying for. God wants the prodigal to come home, so our job is to be there on the journey.

4

The Little Yes

THE LITTLE YES: making an intentional decision to look into the Christian faith; this can be to God or simply to oneself.

It was a mid-week day in summer about fifteen years ago and I had just ended one of my Reason to Believe courses. In this course we ask if it is reasonable to believe in view of the many objections to the Christian faith. The course is aimed at giving people an opportunity to look into the Christian faith and on the final night, after we have taken them on a journey, an opportunity is given to say a BIG YES to God.

It was my usual approach to the response which is conversational and relaxed. I ended with the words, "If you said yes to God tonight I would love to offer you one of my booklets," (it's called *The Journey* and is written for people who have just said yes to God). "I will be by the door. Just come and see me on your way out and I would love to give you a copy." I'd been by the door and a number of guests had come to see me asking for a booklet. One such lady came to see me; she was in her mid-twenties. She looked very happy as she came towards me, which is always encouraging. She said, "Mark, I've really enjoyed attending these talks, I would love to have one of your booklets, if that's okay?"

"Of course it is," I said as I passed it to her. I asked my usual question so that I can understand where people are at, "Did you say yes to God this evening?"

"Oh no," she said, "I said yes to God about two years ago. I said yes to Christianity this evening."

I found her answer intriguing. When she told me she said yes to God two years ago my mind initially thought that maybe she was what we would have called a "backslidden" Christian back in the day and that maybe she had given her life back to God that evening. I had clearly got that wrong! The next part of the conversation was very revealing and taught me something very valuable. I said to her, "I am so glad that you said yes to Jesus and his death on the cross for you." On the final night of Reason to Believe we look at whether it is reasonable to believe that Christianity is right and it's at this stage where we look at the birth, life, death and resurrection of Jesus, presenting the gospel more explicitly and clearly. It's always on the basis of Jesus, with who he is and what he did, that I encourage people to say yes to God. It was therefore a fair assumption I'd made from my theological perspective that her embracing Christianity was therefore embracing Jesus – I mean, let's face it, there is a link. However, this wasn't the case in her mind as she said to me, "Oh I didn't say yes to Jesus, I just said yes to Christianity." I mean, what do you do? Ask her for the booklet back! I didn't, by the way, I simply said how glad I was that she had said yes to God and now to Christianity and I encouraged her to not leave it too long before she said yes to Jesus, and saying yes to him would make sense of her decision that night and arguably the one of two years previous.

The lessons I learnt from that night and many other nights which stay with me in my evangelism and preaching and working with local churches can be summed as:

> 1. A Big Yes in *our* minds is more often than not another Little Yes in the mind of the person on a journey towards God.
>
> 2. For some people the bigger decision they make may not be a theological one; it may be a psychological one i.e. a willingness to look into the Christian faith.
>
> 3. It can, more often than not, take people many times to hear the gospel and process the gospel and accept the gospel.
>
> 4. It's important that we don't see the Big Yes as the end of the journey. The Big Yes is about starting the next phase of the journey!
>
> 5. When someone says a Big Yes it doesn't automatically mean they have fully understood everything about the gospel.

I have said it many times but want to reiterate that I still believe in the Big Yes moments and that there are people gifted in leading seekers through this, but I still believe it's important for the sake of those who aren't ready to say the Big Yes but who most certainly aren't saying a big no, that we create a multi-level response to the gospel. I mentioned about the *encounter* conversions in the last chapter but I want to focus a bit more on the *thinking* conversion in this chapter but of course there is overlap.

I am sure, like me, you admire C.S. Lewis who has to be up there as one of the greatest authors ever. His ability to write such amazing books in *The Chronicles of Narnia*, globally enjoyed by children and adults, is astonishing. Add to this, books like *Mere Christianity* and *The Problem of Pain* to name just a couple, Lewis is definitely someone worth reading. But just how did he become a Christian?

> *Lewis and fellow novelist J.R.R. Tolkien were close friends. They both served on the English faculty at Oxford University, and were active in the informal Oxford literary group known as the Inklings. According to Lewis's memoir* Surprised by Joy, *he was baptised in the Church of Ireland, but fell away from his faith during adolescence.*
>
> *After his conversion to theism in 1929, Lewis converted to Christianity in 1931, following a long discussion and late-night walk with his close friends Tolkien and Hugo Dyson. He records making a specific commitment to Christian belief while on his way to the zoo with his brother. He became a member of the Church of England – somewhat to the disappointment of Tolkien, who had hoped that he would join the Catholic Church.*[8]

C.S. Lewis definitely falls in the Little Yes camp. Notice he converted to theism before he converted to Christianity, similar to the lady's story at the beginning of this chapter.

I can't remember exactly when but it must have been twenty years ago that I first came across Engel's scale; it's quite well known these days. It's been such a liberating thing for many as it seeks to help us visually understand the faith journey. I have always liked it and found it helpful. My only criticism of it (and it's more how we respond to it as opposed to the scale itself) is that we have largely accepted that this is how people come to faith but we have left is as a passive thing and not an active thing i.e. if that is how people come to faith we should base our evangelism on it! Well this was my thinking as I started, once I had seen it help churches do just that. It was thanks to Engel's scale that Big Yes, Little Yes, Healthy Maybe was born. I have inserted Engel's scale here for you to reference and then I will make a few observations in the context of Little Yes.

Engel's Scale[9]

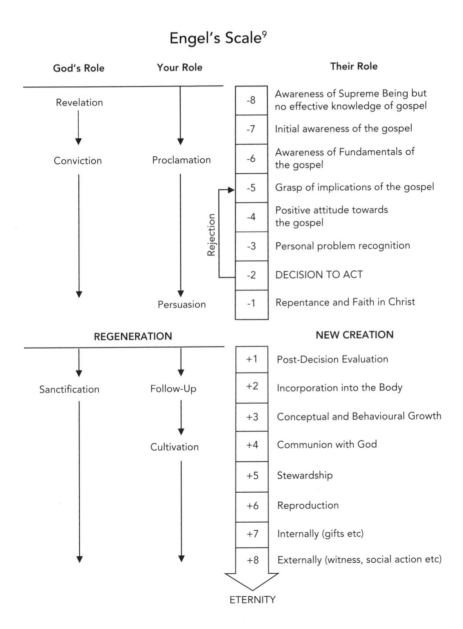

God's Role	Your Role			Their Role
Revelation		-8		Awareness of Supreme Being but no effective knowledge of gospel
		-7		Initial awareness of the gospel
Conviction	Proclamation	-6		Awareness of Fundamentals of the gospel
		-5		Grasp of implications of the gospel
		-4	Rejection	Positive attitude towards the gospel
		-3		Personal problem recognition
		-2		DECISION TO ACT
	Persuasion	-1		Repentance and Faith in Christ

REGENERATION — **NEW CREATION**

Sanctification	Follow-Up	+1	Post-Decision Evaluation
		+2	Incorporation into the Body
	Cultivation	+3	Conceptual and Behavioural Growth
		+4	Communion with God
		+5	Stewardship
		+6	Reproduction
		+7	Internally (gifts etc)
		+8	Externally (witness, social action etc)

ETERNITY

1. God's Role, Your Role

Engel's scale seeks to show the three people involved in a person coming to faith. Now we have already said quite a bit about God's role and our role so I don't intend to say too much here about that apart from this brilliant verse from the Bible: "Since, then, we know what it is to fear the Lord, we try to persuade others" (2 Corinthians 5:11). The Greek word here incidentally for "persuade" means "by sweetness to convince", I love that as coupled with, "For we are to God the pleasing aroma of Christ among those who are being saved and those who are perishing" (2 Corinthians 2:15) we clearly have a role of representing God to those who don't know him, which again is a privilege.

- **God's role:** the scale shows that God has to reveal himself and convict them of their need of him. The regeneration and new creation refers to them becoming a Christian and then the sanctification is the cleaning up bit!

- **Your role:** we get to proclaim and persuade (this is about sharing our faith and journeying) and then when they receive Christ we follow them up and the cultivation refers to helping them to grow by receiving and giving i.e. serving God's kingdom with their gifts as well as leading others.

2. Their Role

You will see from the scale that it starts at -8 and ends at +8. Now don't get too fixated by that, there are certainly times when the matrix doesn't neatly fit onto the trajectory of a person's journey; there are some that are pre -8 but let me position this as for those who are Little Yes people as opposed to the whole conversion arc.

The key thing to notice here is the phases that people go through which again fit into what my friend Duncan explained to us:

-8 to -6

Quite general here with no real obvious moving towards the Christian faith. This could be just a passive interest. People may have their perceptions of

God and Christianity/Christians changed. This could be more around the Healthy Maybe. There may be a touch of the Little Yes here i.e. a person may look into it but not necessarily because they have a real pulling or wanting to investigate in terms of finding out whether God is real.

-5 to -2

This is really where the Little Yes kicks in. This can be quite frustrating, you can see ground gained and ground lost. This part of the journey can often be the longest as it takes a person from believing generally to believing personally and the implications of that are big.

Have you ever had a conversation with someone and it's gone really well? You may have even said to yourself or a friend, "They aren't far from the kingdom," and then you see them again and you now think you must have dreamed it! That's what is happening here.

As I said earlier, most people go through accepting – rejecting – accepting – rejecting many times before they finally embrace the Christian faith.

-1 to +8

But the journey doesn't stop there. From -1 to +8 it continues to be a journey. The moments from -1 to +1 are so crucial. I produced a booklet called *The Journey* for people who have said the Big Yes to God and the first couple of pages deal with "Was it real or was it just me?" I would argue that for many people that is the first thing they think within days of saying the Big Yes. It's the post-decision valuation. It is part of the human brain but also the spiritual battle. These are important moments and we need to walk closely with people during this time. In truth this continues throughout the Christian journey but for most of us we learn how to deal with it or it dissipates.

Going back to that whole exercise thing, I feel so great when I have been to the gym or for a run. As I stand in the shower feeling so clean inside, I am definitely going to keep doing this. In fact, do you know what? I'm going to sign up for a half marathon. The following day, I'm not so keen! The key thing about this stage is we cannot rush it with people but so often we can be focused on the big stuff that we don't see the little steps. When my kids first started walking and I stood just a few steps away, the fact they didn't make it all the way to me didn't matter because it was just lovely to see them taking that first step.

Lessons from the Chinese Bamboo Tree

This might not be the first time you have heard this told but I am going to tell you it anyway! It is such a great lesson to learn.

The Chinese bamboo tree is one of the strongest trees in the world, surviving harsh weather conditions. Bamboo is used to build roads and bridges as well as scaffolding as it is incredibly durable, strong and able to support a large amount of weight. You will find plenty of bamboo bridges in India and Cambodia. It is environmentally friendly and in Hong Kong it is much more popular than metal scaffolding. Bamboo can be easily bent but is very difficult to break and so it is widely used in the construction of fishing equipment. In countries like Vietnam, fishing boats are also made of bamboo. They are extremely light and very easy to manoeuvre. Bamboo is water resistant and these bamboo boats allow the fishermen to enter into narrow channels where commercial boats can't enter. I'm sure you will agree that Bamboo is amazing, but consider this ...

The Chinese bamboo tree grows eighty-feet tall in just six weeks! However, it's only in its fifth year that this incredible growth takes place. It appears that nothing happens for those first four years and yet if at any time in those years the watering and fertilising process is stopped, the Chinese bamboo tree will die in the ground.

Question: Did the Chinese bamboo tree grow eighty feet in five years or six weeks?

Answer: In five years.

We need to be patient and prayerful in all the seasons of people's journey but I guess the Little Yes season can be long and frustrating and can sometimes look like nothing is happening.

Another thing to highlight here has been hinted at already and was true for C.S. Lewis as well as the lady at Reason to Believe. A person could be Big Yes about God but Little Yes about Jesus or even Healthy Maybe about him. Another person could be Big Yes about Jesus but Little Yes about God. They could even be Big Yes about receiving Jesus but Little Yes about repentance. This is why in the discipleship journey in Chapter 2 as well as implicit throughout the book, it's important for personal pathway and not just collective course. You see Big Yes, Little Yes, Healthy Maybe has a psychological dynamic to it as well as a theological dynamic. It's just not as binary as we would love it to be. I go back to the lady at Reason to Believe who accepted Christianity before she accepted Jesus. Theologically there may be a problem but not in her mind.

The Little Yes season can be long and frustrating and can sometimes look like nothing is happening.

My favourite time of the year is the six nations. For the non-initiated it's a Rugby Union tournament where England (my team), Wales, Ireland, Scotland, France and Italy all play against each other. It happens every year over February and March and is the highlight of my sporting year. Every year it kicks off at the beginning of February, which happens to be my birthday and so, complete with my bottle of Cherry Pepsi Max and my favourite sweets Midget Gems (has to be the hard ones not the cheap ones), I take a deep breath and the adrenaline kicks in. It's tense and I get more emotionally invested in it than I should. My family are very kind as I like to watch and not really talk.

One particular year, just as the national anthems were coming to an end, my wife Emma came in to the sitting room. "Can you plant these ten plants for me, please, this afternoon? I'm off out and I will be back later on."

"Sure," I said, as I worked out there would be enough time at half time if I was quick to get them in. I thought maximum one per minute. Half time arrived and I was up, out, and back in the chair as the two teams ran back onto the pitch. "Boom," I said in celebration of a job well done or, more importantly, quickly done.

Emma arrived back and asked me if I had made a start on the plants. "Start," I said, "it is finished," I announced with a pause between each word, denoting a mild sense of victory which I had hoped would deal with Emma's tone of doubt as she posed the question.

Several minutes later she returned to the room and said, "Can you come outside please?" It was at this moment that I ceased to feel the confident forty-year-old man I was at the time and as she led me to every plant, moving it with her feet very easily, saying the words, "That needs re-doing ... that needs re-doing ..." and so it went on. "You haven't even watered them in." I assured her I didn't need to as the weather forecast tomorrow showed it was going to throw it down. She explained each plant needed to be watered in and how I needed to follow the instructions as each plant was different. I was going to say, "Why didn't you tell me so?" when she said the words, "You were so keen to plant everything but you planted nothing." Ouch, she was right: my priority was just to get the plants in without any thoughts about how best to plant them.

Often in our evangelism we can be so keen to plant everything about the gospel without planting anything. We often get an opportunity to share that we weren't expecting and we end up doing what I call "panic preaching". In other words, we blurt it all out without any real thought or sensitivity. It would be better to plant one thing well which actually often leads to being able to share more. With my friends I try to create journey rather than arrive at a dead end.

My friend Laurence Singlehurst has written a brilliant book called *Sowing, Reaping, Keeping*.[10] I have to say that Laurence and I certainly have synergy in what we believe about evangelism. I would definitely recommend you read it.

In his book he talks about evangelism in the context of one-on-one. I love the concept here where he talks about driving a five-ton truck across a one-ton bridge, illustrating that we can expect too much too quickly. He says, "We can also see how our expectations affect our one-to-one relationships. Because of our misunderstanding of sowing and reaping, we have a tendency to expect too much too quickly. So it is essential that we understand the process that people have to go through before they can make a proper decision for Christ." He goes onto say, "So what should we do? Well, perhaps it would be better for us to recognise that we have a formative relationship and to break down our five-ton gospel message, as it were, into five one-ton messages. Then over a period of time we can help them across."[11]

I want to encourage you to build the relationships with your friends and trust the relationships with your friends. When you build quality relationships there will be no shortage of time to share and unpack and plant the gospel well. You don't need to worry about them being run down by a bus!

Big Yes or Final Little Yes?

What is also interesting in this Little Yes season is that I have seen so many times people who haven't quite said the Big Yes yet suddenly start to get involved in the life of the church. It is in this season that a greater sense of belonging takes place and even their behaviour changes. I've seen them get involved in serving the church and even praying. When a person comes through this stage and says the Big Yes it is often the final Little Yes for them. What we have been praying for and thinking may never happen, has often been more a case of "when, not if". I have seen this happen so much and even as I write this book a few ministers have shared with me how they have had this happen in their churches with people who have been on some of the events and courses I had done with them. I love it.

The Spiritual Dynamic – the Enemy

I don't understand a great deal about spiritual warfare, if I'm honest, but I do believe God showed me something many years ago: there is never a more intense moment of spiritual activity in the heavenly realms than at the moment a person is considering Christ.

I have talked a lot about the human side of a person coming to Christ and I am totally convinced about that for all sorts of reasons – many of which I have already discussed in this book. The truth is I have a lot more to say about that because that's my expertise and I feel God has spoken to me loads about it. What I do want to say at this point, however, is we should never underestimate the spiritual side of it either. That's partly why in Chapter 1 I talked about a lack of God's power. We can put lots in place and yet miss the prayer dynamic. What I would say is hopefully now you can begin to pray with understanding about the process by which people come to faith. A prayer I have long prayed is straight from the Bible – I love praying the scripture!

> *Devote yourselves to prayer, being watchful and thankful. And pray for us, too, that God may open a door for our message, so that we may proclaim the mystery of Christ, for which I am in chains. Pray that I may proclaim it clearly, as I should. Be wise in the way you act towards outsiders; make the most of every opportunity. Let your conversation be always full of grace, seasoned with salt, so that you may know how to answer everyone. (Colossians 2:4–6)*

What a great verse this is – it seems to marry together the fact that we need to be the best we can, do the best we can, speak the best we can and ask that God does all he can. Why not use this as a mission prayer.

#WeCan'tCreateSoulsButWeCanCreateJourney

Journey

Unable to shake off the words, "You're listening to the wrong radio station," Liam Husband began to realise he had been listening to all the wrong influences and had never given God a thought.

I sat down all alone in my shared house and the words came back to me. They weren't my words; they were the lyrics of a song that had come into my head just a few days earlier as I was walking home and here they were again – they never stopped. "You're listening to the wrong radio station," but this time they started to make sense.

All the time whilst following my peers, doing what I thought was cool, pursuing what I thought would make me happy, I had been listening to the wrong message, the wrong radio station. It hit me between the eyes in an instant – God wanted to talk to me. He was available if I chose to listen to him rather than the million other messages firing round at the same time.

I'd never given God much thought until that day, and if I had it meant so little to me. God was distant. He wasn't a God I knew or recognised. I'd like to say that moment changed my life and the very next day I woke up a completely different person, but I didn't. I was on a subutex prescription for heroin addiction. I was still trying to get my life together. I was still living in my past: a cycle of addiction, violence and prison. I was visiting my case worker everyday and working towards rehab. For once I'd had enough of the never-ending cycle of misery and was desperate for change.

Not long after having the first thoughts about God wanting to speak to me I recall another evening when something deep went on within me. I was on my own in my house, watching a film. I can't remember what film it was but I do remember I was half listening and half concentrating on writing in my notebook when I heard a phrase that resonated within me: "Give something to get something." Again those words just rang and grabbed me so much that I wrote them down at the top of a blank page. I then began to repeatedly write them down whilst almost meditating over them – "Give something to get something" – as if each time I wrote the phrase down I was getting a clearer understanding of what it meant to me. I had to give something to get something. But what? My life! I had to give my life? But how? Why? And to what? I realised I had to give my life away to get my life. I can't explain what was really going on but by the end of the page I had written, "I am on a journey to meet my maker." Something in me, my mind, my soul, was changing. It's as if a light that I had covered for so long with my addiction was finding its way out. From an angry addict with no understanding of God or anything spiritual to a genuine feeling of awakening but confused as to what.

About two months later I found myself in the middle of nowhere on a farm in Shropshire. I had managed to get into a rehab. The appeal for me was a trip to South America and leaving the farm with enough qualifications to build a new life – I even got a chainsaw licence! I struggled to settle at first. It was a whole new experience for me but I made some great relationships with some great people. All the staff had something very different about them which I had never seen anywhere else – it made me curious. A peace, a joy, a genuine love for each other, something I had been searching for all my life was apparent in these people, and I wanted it.

I started a journey of discovery that day. I went to church because these people went to church. I listened to what was said, sung and prayed, and I dipped in and out. It didn't all make sense, I had no blinding revelation of light overnight but the more I journeyed with them the more it made sense. I learned about a man called Jesus who was the Son of God and how I could have a relationship with him. I heard that I could be forgiven for all the things I had done to people in my past and that he would help me change to be the person I was so desperate to be. So I made a choice: I wanted to know Jesus, I wanted to be a Christian because of everything I had seen in the past few months. I knew that there was something in it but I

couldn't put my finger on it exactly. I remember going to a church event one evening at a local school. The preacher made a call at the end for anyone who wanted to be a Christian. I'd seen enough to know I wanted in, so I said yes and was prayed for.

For almost a month I had no idea if I was a Christian or not. I would go to sleep every night repeating the phrase, "Jesus, I let you into my life." I never woke up feeling different but I kept on saying it until I fell asleep every night. I worked through my rehab programme and did all I could to get to know Jesus. I read my Bible, I went to prayer meetings, I went to Alpha, I asked hundreds of questions and slowly for me the jigsaw started to take shape and, before I knew it, I was six months drug free! I hadn't been six months drug free since the age of ten. I felt different, life felt different; in fact everything felt different. At the end of my programme I went off to South America and was baptised in the Rupununi River in Guyana. I wanted the old me to stay in South America; I was ready for the new me to start – a whole new life. Once I got back and finished my rehab I went off to Bible school to learn more. I ended up working in the same rehab and then started to train as a minister.

I now serve in a local church in Bournemouth and I love the life I was given by Jesus. I'm so grateful someone introduced me to Jesus by living a life that showed what it meant to be a Christian – that was enough for me. I live a life now that I never thought was possible and it all started with those lyrics, "You're listening to the wrong radio station."

5

The Healthy Maybe

THE HEALTHY MAYBE: willing to become or remain open minded – maybe there is something in this.

It was one of many conversations that I had with my brother-in-law at the time. To be honest he had some valid points as he had made marketing a pretty successful and financially rewarding profession. "The problem you face, Mark," he would say, "is that the church has the most famous product in the world (God) but the worst branding and marketing (Christians and the church)." Whilst I debated the point about God being a product I did say to him that he had some valid thoughts. He said to me, "You talk about the Bible being God's word and yet it looks so drab." It was this statement that made me create my *Look Closer: Mark's Gospel.*[12]

One of the biggest challenges the church faces is changing the perceptions people have of the Christian faith. It's important to know that there is an increasing opinion that the church is outdated let alone even thinking about what it thinks about God. I believe that we have to position a lot more of our evangelism in the Healthy Maybe if we are to connect with people. This doesn't mean that we minimise the other elements we have just covered in the previous two chapters; no I believe we have to increase it all but we have to spend some time developing our fringe.

I'd finished one of my "Comedy and Christianity" events and I was approached by an older gentleman who had been invited by his family. The aim of such an event is to seek to change the perception that people have of the Christian faith. Off the back of these events people are often invited to come along to hear me speak on a Sunday morning some six weeks later or to attend an Alpha or my Reason to Believe course.

One of the biggest challenges the church faces is changing the perceptions people have of the Christian faith.

Back to the gentleman. I could see him heading towards me as I stood at the door. As I chatted to him he told me how much he had enjoyed the evening and that he would come and see the event that was advertised on the postcard on the table. He was intrigued as to how I would preach and use humour as opposed to doing a comedy routine. True to his word, he came along and actually on that morning came to faith in Christ. I met him a further six months on and he came to see me with the biggest smile ever, announcing, "I'm still going strong you know, I've been to church every Sunday and I've now done Alpha!" It was lovely to see. This is one of many reasons I value, celebrate and encourage what I call the "healthy maybe" in a person's journey to faith.

Could This Be?

There is no single passage that has had greater impact on me in my personal evangelism than that of John chapter 4 where Jesus was having a conversation with a woman at a well. For my narrative I quote here verses 27–42 which picks up just after the disciples rejoin Jesus having gone off to get some food ...

Just then his disciples returned and were surprised to find him talking with a woman. But no one asked, "What do you want?" or "Why are you talking with her?" Then, leaving her water jar, the woman went back to the town and said to the people, "Come, see a man who told me everything I've ever done. Could this be the Messiah?" They came out of the town and made their way toward him. Meanwhile his disciples urged him, "Rabbi, eat something." But he said to them, "I have food to eat that you know nothing about." Then his disciples said to each other, "Could someone have brought him food?"

"My food," said Jesus, "is to do the will of him who sent me and to finish his work. Don't you have a saying, 'It's still four months until harvest'? I tell you, open your eyes and look at the fields! They are ripe for harvest. Even now the one who reaps draws a wage and harvests a crop for eternal life, so that the sower and the reaper may be glad together. Thus the saying 'One sows and another reaps' is true. I sent you to reap what you have not worked for. Others have done the hard work, and you have reaped the benefits of their labour."

Many of the Samaritans from that town believed in him because of the woman's testimony, "He told me everything I've ever done." So when the Samaritans came to him, they urged him to stay with them, and he stayed two days. And because of his words many more became believers. They said to the woman, "We no longer believe just because of what you said; now we have heard for ourselves, and we know that this man really is the Saviour of the world."

Notice with me a couple of things:

1. **When she leaves Jesus** just as after the disciples return, she is so impacted she leaves the water jar – renewed priorities kick in and she says, "Come, see a man who told me everything I've ever done. Could this be the Messiah?" She is presenting a Healthy Maybe to her community. I don't think she fully knows herself yet. I have known people who attend my Reason to Believe course who have invited their friends to come along even though they haven't fully decided yet – love it.

   In verse 39 we are told that many believed in him because of that woman's testimony. You can't find anywhere in the life of Jesus where that many people become his followers. And to think he was tired from the journey, hungry and thirsty and probably just wanted to rest. O Lord, in my everyday, help me create Healthy Maybes!

2. **Something really interesting** takes place. Those who believed said, "We no longer believe just because of what you said; now we have heard for ourselves, and we know that this man really is the Saviour of the world." They looked into it and in doing so seemed to discover a greater truth than the Samaritan woman – this man wasn't just the Messiah (the saviour of the Jews) but rather the Saviour of the world. They were definitely Little Yes people. All this from someone who said, "Could this be?"

All this happened because Jesus was real, he even asked for help when he was in need himself! It didn't happen as a result of any planned evangelism but rather as the result of Jesus doing normal life! Now there's a lesson to learn. So often we think we are the ones who have to do everything but maybe the real power in relationships is when we invite people into our needs, as Jesus did, before we try to meet theirs. That brings real dignity and connectivity.

This isn't the only "come and see, could this be" moment in the Gospels.

> *The next day Jesus decided to leave for Galilee. Finding Philip, he said to him, "Follow me."*
>
> *Philip, like Andrew and Peter, was from the town of Bethsaida. Philip found Nathanael and told him, "We have found the one Moses wrote about in the Law, and about whom the prophets also wrote – Jesus of Nazareth, the son of Joseph."*
>
> *"Nazareth! Can anything good come from there?" Nathanael asked.*
>
> *"Come and see," said Philip.* (John 1:43–46)

Not quite as many responding but still great. Come and see for yourself!

Let me remind you at this stage of the Talking Jesus research that revealed that approximately 1 in 5 adults and 1 in 6 young people are interested in an encounter with Jesus, and the same are interested in finding out more about him. Here we have it: encounter and thinking – and both age groups are at least Healthy Maybe and possibly Little Yes.

Okay so the research reveals there are people who aren't interested in an encounter or finding out more but let's concern ourselves with where God may be at work or where there is good soil.

A community of Healthy Maybes!

My very good friend Revd Andy Lenton is Community Pastor at Bridge Community Church in Leeds. In the heart of a challenging area the church gets on average about 1000 people every Sunday. As well as a good evangelistic rhythm they have some extensive community work going through the week. I asked Andy what he thought about "Healthy Maybe". He wrote:

ANDY LENTON

For approximately six years we have leased a small unit in our local shopping parade. It's a sad but typical mixture of outlets: cash-converters, betting shops, laundrette, bargain booze and chemist. Sad because four of the units feed an ever-growing population of addiction; whether it's alcohol, crime, gambling or prescription drugs they all add to the deprivation figures that make this area of Leeds one of the poorest and most deprived in the country. So, we call our little unit "The Welcome".

It's a place where a dedicated and compassionate team welcome anyone and everyone who needs help or a listening ear and, along with a warm cuppa, they are offered simple prayer. It's not "in your face" evangelism but "love your neighbour" type stuff and, as a result, we have seen a steady flow of people helped into rehab or beginning to come to our Sunday services. But there are some that are happy to receive prayer but cannot see the relevance of what we call our "worship service". This causes us to think "out of the box" because the fact that individuals are open to prayer encourages us to believe they are expressing a "healthy maybe" and we just need to find the next step that will help them a little further down the road towards a relationship with Jesus.

Easter last year saw us putting on all the usual "celebration" style meetings to gather the faithful but we also took the risk and booked a night of wrestling calling it "The Greatest Battle". Announcing it in church brought me much discouragement because it seemed like no one was coming and the night would be a flop. But as the start time drew near we were amazed to see 500 people coming from the local community into the church building. The evening was truly a "knockout": bout after bout of full-blooded wrestling culminating in a powerful testimony by one of the wrestlers. Thirty people responding to the gospel appeal with many more taking away literature or signing up for the Alpha course.

It has caused us to think seriously about how many people are on our doorstep carrying a "healthy maybe" and how we can convert that into a "yes", either big or little.

I remember speaking to a lady who was disappointed and defeated because her husband didn't commit to following Jesus at a particular event I was speaking at. She had been praying for him for thirty years! Yet that night was the first night he had come along to church with her and he had asked her if he could come. That's a Healthy Maybe! It might not have been the Big Yes but it needed to be celebrated.

If you ever listen to someone telling you their story of how they came to faith in Christ – most people's journey involved them at some point travelling through the Healthy Maybe on their way to a Little Yes and a Big Yes. I've met so many people when they've been in the Healthy Maybe stage. It excites me because at this stage they are on the way. If we're not careful we can put such a big focus on a person committing their life to Christ that we end up not celebrating all the little decisions along the way. This means anything that helps address this, however small, is something we should celebrate. Whenever I preach the gospel, share my faith one-to-one, produce resources or help churches with their evangelism, I try to build in a Healthy Maybe option. I've had people come to see me at the end of my evangelistic events introducing themselves as "a healthy maybe" – this makes me happy as they are on the way!

Have a prayerful think about the people with whom you have had the opportunity to share your faith. Are any of them a Healthy Maybe or Little Yes or Big Yes? What can you do to help them along that journey?

We have tended to position our evangelism in the Big Yes but I hope that through reading this book you can see we need to change this somewhat. I believe we need to position our evangelism in the Healthy Maybe. Let's take seriously changing the perceptions people have of the Christian faith.

A Friend, a Wife, a Hospital and a Book

Big Yes, Little Yes, Healthy Maybe can be as much psychological as it can be theological. A person's willingness to look into the Christian faith might be a big psychological decision as opposed to a theological decision! I've known many an atheist look into Christianity not because they are thinking about becoming a Christian but because they think they ought to. Indeed one of my friends, Pete, looked into Christianity because his wife (who wasn't a Christian) said to him you ought to be as fair to Christianity, and put as much time into researching it, as you do evolution and science.

From a young age Pete studied science, reading books on evolution, genetics, medical science and physics. He had the answers to life and was sure that his opinion was obviously correct. Then he met a Christian. He thought he was going to test him and catch him out and so over the next two years they exchanged questions and answers. Pete noticed that his friend seemed to be sorted with his life, not shouting or complaining.

Pete's son had to have an operation. There was a key moment for him when his Christian friend said, "I will pray for you, your son and family." That statement changed his view of Christians; he instantly felt that his friend really and genuinely cared for Pete and his family. The love that his friend had shown towards him and his family had a lasting effect on him.

Whilst in the hospital Pete bought the Alpha book *Searching Issues* by Nicky Gumbel, and after the operation (which went well) he started to read it. This is when Pete's wife said he must give the same chance to Christianity as he had to science and that he should have a balanced view, and not a view of Christianity from the bias of science. He found a hunger to read it and couldn't get enough. It all made sense as he read about the historical evidence for Jesus, and as he understood why Jesus died he said the sinner's prayer.

He quite unexpectedly felt something like a surge of energy within his body which he couldn't explain. His life changed that day and he felt free, unchained and full of faith that God is the Creator; he was completely satisfied and at peace. All this because someone was kind, gave good answers and prayed for Pete.

I know of many who are Christians today who came to one of my Healthy Maybe events and as per the challenge from me to "afford yourself the luxury of looking into Christianity – have a proper look, don't be a person who has decided they don't want it without really knowing what it is they aren't wanting."

For me Big Yes, Little Yes, Healthy Maybe is not just a buzz word but a biblical principle, historical precedent and the way that most people come to faith.

As local churches we need to do a lot more in the Healthy Maybe element and, of course, connect it all together which I will address in Part 2 of this book.

#WeCan'tCreateSoulsButWeCanCreateJourney

Notes

Notes

Notes

PART

2

INTRODUCTION

A Restricted Mentality

A number of years ago I came across this bit of information and I have to admit it made me chuckle. On the side of the Space Shuttle there are two solid rocket boosters, or SRBs. They were the first solid fuel motors to be used for primary propulsion on a vehicle used for human space flight and they provided the majority of the Space Shuttle's thrust during the first two minutes of flight. After burnout, they were jettisoned and parachuted into the Atlantic Ocean from where they were recovered, examined, refurbished and reused.

The SRBs are made at a factory in Utah. The engineers who designed the SRBs wanted to make them a bit fatter, but the SRBs had to be shipped by train from the factory to the launch site. The railroad line to the factory runs through a tunnel in the mountains. The SRBs had to fit through that tunnel. The tunnel is slightly wider than a railroad track, and the railroad track is about as wide as two horses' behinds.

The US standard railroad gauge (distance between the rails) is 4 feet 8.5 inches. That's the way they built them in England, and the US railroads were built by English expatriates. Why did the English people build them like that? Because the first rail lines were built by the same people who built the pre-railroad tramways, and that's the gauge they used. Why did they use that gauge then? Because the people who built the tramways used the same jigs and tools that they used for building wagons, which used that wheel spacing. Why did the wagons use that odd wheel spacing? Well, if they tried to use any other spacing the wagons would break on some of the old, long-distance roads. The first long-distance roads in Europe were built by Imperial Rome for the benefit of their legions and their chariots. Since the chariots were made for or by Imperial Rome they were all alike in the matter of wheel spacing. The roads have been used ever since. The

United States standard railroad gauge of 4 feet 8.5 inches comes from the original specification for an Imperial Roman Army war chariot. The reason? Because that accommodates the back ends of the two horses that pulled the chariot.

Wow, so the goal of sending the Space Shuttle into space was hugely restricted by practices that were carried out about two thousand years ago. We need to make sure we aren't restricting ourselves by what we have done in the past. We need to be prepared to ask the bigger questions of what is and what isn't working in our local churches and be prepared to change.

A Winning Mentality

My former brother-in-law was part of the England rugby coaching staff with Clive Woodward. He did the analysis of the game and produced a detailed report for Clive on each game. When England won the World Cup in 2003 Clive Woodward had managed to create a team that was hard to beat – a very different team from the one he had inherited. We beat the All Blacks and the Australians in their own back yard. I asked my brother-in-law what had happened to get to that place. He said very simply that we had gone from a losing mentality to a winning mentality.

We definitely need to move from a losing mentality in our churches to a wining mentality. Having been involved in seeing this happen in many churches I am confident we can do it. When Clive Woodward started employing a huge backroom staff it raised a lot of eyebrows. Why? Because it hadn't been done before; he was prepared to do something different and a bit radical.

A Looking Mentality

When both my girls were young it was always lovely to see the delight on their faces when they found a coin on the way to school. It was outside the One Stop shop that they were at their most prolific as there were lots of nooks and crannies on the path where the tarmac had degenerated over the years (they were devastated when the path was resurfaced). As they began to find more and more coins the intensity of the competition increased. Once we found a one-pound coin. I felt excited then but thought it un-fatherly to use my weight advantage! Not only did the competition increase but so did the heightened level of expectancy. In other words, they began to leave the house in full anticipation of finding a lost coin. They weren't bothered about the value, they simply wanted to find the lost item and they expected to find one.

I love the Parable of the Lost Coin in Luke 15:8–10.

> *Suppose a woman has ten silver coins and loses one. Doesn't she light a lamp, sweep the house and search carefully until she finds it? And when she finds it, she calls her friends and neighbours together and says, "Rejoice with me; I have found my lost coin." In the same way, I tell you, there is rejoicing in the presence of the angels of God over one sinner who repents.*

It nestles in those three great parables that remind us that God is always looking for the lost. I particularly love the "light a lamp, sweep the house and search carefully until she finds it"; the sense of her being focused and intentional and not stopping until she finds it. This is not a surprise when you do a bit of study and discover this is not some accidentally lost coin that fell out of a pocket as a tissue was being pulled out. It was the sort of precious coin that would have been in a headdress for a marriage. It had value and story to it, neither of which she wanted to lose. When we think about those who are lost let's see the story and the value and do all we can as local churches to find them.

I've already quoted from 2 Corinthians 5 and I would like to again. It's another one of those life passages I mentioned. In particular I want to draw this amazing phrase to you, which is found in verse 16: "So from now on we regard no one from a worldly point of view." Let's be determined to view no one from a worldly point of view but to see all as valuable and findable.

Yes, But How?

The bestselling types of books are the "How to ..." books. Incidentally the bestselling of those are cookbooks showing you how to cook amazing food. The next bestselling after that are diet books! That's right, showing you how to lose the weight you have just put on because of all the cook books you have bought and used!

My friend J.John tells of when he first became a Christian he heard lots of talks that challenged him and he would often write in his Bible "YBH". These letters stood for "Yes, but how?" In other words, yes I agree but show me how I can do it.

Big Yes, Little Yes, Healthy Maybe is nothing other than a framework wherein we can see where people are at and help them move along the journey without forcing them to make a decision they aren't ready to make. It prevents us from putting wrong and unnecessary pressure on ourselves. This will, I believe, help establish a winning mentality and not a losing mentality. In Part 2 we are going to look at the "Yes, but how?"

#WeCan'tCreateSoulsButWeCanCreateJourney

6

Using BYLYHM in Local Church Evangelism

The Choluteca Bridge in Honduras, also known as the Bridge of Rising Sun, was built by Hazama Ando Corporation between 1996 and 1998 and became the largest bridge constructed by a Japanese company in Latin America. In the same year that the bridge was commissioned for use, Honduras was hit by Hurricane Mitch, which caused considerable damage to the nation and its infrastructure. Many bridges were damaged and some were destroyed, but the Choluteca Bridge survived with minor damage. While the bridge itself was in near-perfect condition, the roads on either end of the bridge had completely vanished, leaving no visible

trace of their prior existence. More impressively, the Choluteca River (which is several hundred feet wide) had carved itself a new channel during the massive flooding caused by the hurricane. It no longer flowed beneath the bridge, which now spanned dry ground. The bridge quickly became known as "The Bridge to Nowhere". In 2003, the bridge was reconnected to the highway.

It's good to know that the bridge was eventually reconnected but for several years there was a beautiful, resilient structure that was of no use and quite literally going nowhere. Undeniably the cultural river has changed and the church is struggling to be a bridge, we have some reconnecting to do, some extending to reach into where culture is at as opposed to expecting the culture river to change its course back.

There are three main ways that we can engage people with the gospel in our outreach as local churches:

1. **Friends:** the people we meet on a day-to-day basis.

2. **Overt evangelism:** this would be the likes of open-air work and door-to-door evangelism.

3. **Community engagement:** in terms of churches this is probably the key way that we can impact our communities with the gospel. I talk about this more in Chapter 7.

All of these must have a relational build if they are to be successful. We have to stay connected and attractive or risk being passed by. We need to connect our ethos to all areas so that we have a coherent strategy that is clear in people's minds.

A lot of our local church evangelism in the past has predominated in the Big Yes i.e. given people an opportunity to become Christians. We've got lots of great courses that facilitate the Little Yes i.e. giving people the opportunity to intentionally find out more by investigating. Again, I'm not suggesting for one minute that we stop these or even do less of them, quite the opposite. I would love to see more churches do more of these. What I am suggesting, however, is that we do position our evangelism in the Healthy Maybe by increasing outreach to create that which enables people to become open minded about the Christian faith. We've got a lot of people for whom we need to change their perceptions of God and Christianity. Now it may be that the river of your locality isn't as close to you as you would like so you may need to do a lot more Healthy Maybe stuff at first.

Bubbling-along Evangelism

Here is an events-based strategy to doing evangelism. Many have tried to suggest that this isn't effective but I have to say this is not my experience. Events can do a number of really helpful things:

1. **They supplement** your personal evangelism not replace it.

2. **They provide a way** for your friends to hear the gospel in a way that you aren't able to share. This can be purely through ability i.e. some people are just gifted at getting the message across. There is also the relational tension – it can be hard sharing the hard bits of the gospel with those you are closest to.

3. **They help further discussion** as you can discuss with them what you both heard.

4. **They can provide connection** with other Christians which hopefully is a good thing!

5. **They can provide a useful steppingstone** in the Big Yes, Little Yes, Healthy Maybe.

So taking that all into account I would like to suggest some way forward for you to establish bubbling-along evangelism i.e. evangelism that keeps happening rather than just at big moments.

1. Take the academic year and divide it into the three terms.

2. In each term plan a Healthy Maybe level of event at the beginning of the term. Sunday night live or your café-style event is good for this.

3. In each term plan a Little Yes level of event after the Healthy Maybe event. Christianity Explored, Alpha, Reason to Believe (my course), Jesus the Game Changer or Just10 by J.John.

4. In each term plan a Big Yes level of event after the Little Yes event. Guest services are good. Why not have a baptismal service as one. If you are doing dedications or christenings, make those the Big Yes events. Of course, at all these Big Yes events make sure you do Big Yes, Little Yes, Healthy Maybe appeals (more about that in Chapter 9).

5. At all these events have a really nicely produced and professionally printed A6 postcard at which you invite the people to the next two events. Try to keep everything connected and profiled. Even if one of the events is a ticketed event still promote it at the current event on the flyer. Trust me, from experience it makes a difference.

6. Produce all the events you have planned for the year on a really nicely produced menu and have it professionally printed. Make it look like we are valuing the events.

The aim behind this is that we develop a cyclical rhythm that just happens, it bubbles along. Educate your church members as to the different levels of events so that they know who to bring along to what. I have often heard ministers say to me about an artist or speaker that "they were too heavy" or "there wasn't enough gospel in there". This is caused by a number of factors:

- The minister didn't know what level the artist or speaker operates at.

- The minster didn't communicate what was needed.

- Not every singer is good for evangelistic events. I know this seems strange but just because they sing it doesn't mean they are an evangelist or understand how to communicate to unbelievers through their music.

The aim of the cycle is that you have a multi-access approach to your evangelism which means at various points through the year there is something appropriate to bring guests along to. By the way, they don't all have to happen in your church or all have to be big crowds.

As you develop this you will see some of the same people coming to events as the relationships build – they begin to belong. I've regularly seen non-Christians get involved in setting-down events as well as inviting their friends along to them.

The other thing to be aware of is best illustrated by me filling you in about a conversation I had at one of my Reason to Believe courses a few years ago. I'd done the presentation and the small groups had finished when one of the guests came to see me. He told me he had previously been on Alpha and had loved it but he said it would have been better for him to have done Reason to Believe first. He said, "It's like your course is a pre-Alpha." He went on to say, "Your course starts a bit further back in the process." I was so encouraged by this; here was someone who was very self-aware of where he was on the journey of faith. I was also encouraged because I was saying to churches when you do Reason to Believe, do Alpha as a follow-up because Reason to Believe ends where Alpha starts. It's all about understanding the process and letting it inform us.

The cycle I suggest is an aim, as it may be too much for you to do immediately. Look at what you already do and identify whether it is Big Yes, Little Yes, Healthy Maybe and then look at adding whatever you are missing. I have worked with some churches that have predominated in one of the elements – Healthy Maybe – for many years and they needed to do a season of Little Yes events.

HOPE Rhythm of Mission

I have the joy of being a part of the national leadership team of HOPE. The reason I am on this, quite apart from representing Elim, is because I wholeheartedly believe in what it does. There is great synergy between my bubbling-along evangelism model and that of HOPE's Rhythm of Mission. They have produced a really useful diagram which helps us to engage with the communities we are in.

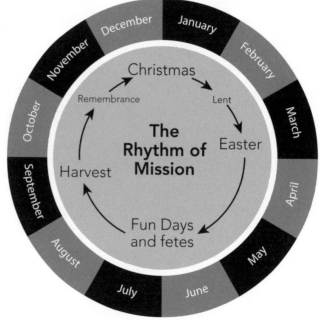

HOPE uses the festivals like Harvest, Remembrance, Easter and Christmas, etc. as a means of reaching our communities. They produce some superb resources to help train and equip your church in faith sharing.

Based on what the Talking Jesus research revealed, HOPE suggests five simple "next steps" which you could use as part of your church evangelism strategy and also as a simple and practical way of helping your church members in their discipleship journey:

1. **Some people to pray for:** identify the 1-in-5 people around you who are open to an encounter with Jesus or open to finding out more about him?

2. **Something to say:** learn how to better share your story and be praying for someone to share it with.

3. **Something to give:** what high-quality booklet or leaflet have you got that you can give away?

4. **An invitation to offer:** is there an event at your church that you could invite someone to? If there isn't, could you put one on?

5. **Someone new to get to know:** who can you get to know?

You can get the full HOPE report which unpacks the Rhythm of Mission some more, including the five points above, from the HOPE Together website (details overleaf).

HOPE is a words-and-actions mission organisation that believes actions and words must be married for effective mission. It shouldn't be an either or, it should be both. You will see in Chapter 7 how Big Yes, Little Yes, Healthy Maybe connects with our social action and community engagement.

The Literature You Use

It's also important to develop this Big Yes, Little Yes, Healthy Maybe approach to the literature we use. I have seen churches give the same booklet to a new Christian as they give to someone who wants to find out more. They also give the same one to someone who needs to be persuaded there is a God. There are lots of great resources out there that are targeted at different levels. Here are a few places you could look:

- www.revmarkgreenwood.com
- www.canonjjohn.com
- www.hopetogether.org.uk
- www.cpo.org.uk

All of these have varied and excellently produced resources that will supplement your Big Yes, Little Yes, Healthy Maybe cycle.

Changing the Culture Takes a While

I am massively into DIY! Okay, so I might not always feel motivated to do it but once I am in the zone I can keep going! I've learned a few little tricks along the way which are brilliant. One such trick was developed when my wife and I bought our very first house – a gorgeous Victorian, double-gabled, bay-windowed end-of-terrace in Bradford. It only cost me £21,000! When it came to fitting a window rail for the curtains in the front bay window there weren't any curved curtain rails available at the DIY store so this is where the trick came in. You shouldn't just bend the rail to fit the shape of the bay as there will always be resistance as you work against the default setting of the rail and therefore heighten the chance that the rail and the curtains won't stay there long term. "So how do you do it?" I can hear you all asking. Well it's simple! You get a hot air gun or hair dryer and gently apply heat and, as you do, you secure the rail to the holders. As the rail cools down the default has changed and so now it all works a treat. The interesting things is that if you now try to fit the rail to a normal non-curved window aperture you have the original problem again whereby the rail will now be under strain as you force it to be something it isn't.

Changing the culture and default setting takes a while. For a culture to be changed and become the new default takes between five and seven years. So don't be disheartened if it takes a while to get going. Keep on and it will come.

I remember a conversation with a minister I had been working with as we partnered together to shift the evangelism culture of the church to a new default. After a number of years we became aware that there were a whole bunch of people now attending the church that had been birthed in what to them was the normal culture of the church. This meant that they were a part of a culture but didn't necessarily understand why it was so. We decided that it would be good to do a kind of "refresher" to remind the original people as well as

For a culture to be changed and become the new default takes between five and seven years.

inform those who were fairly new. The minister announced that I would be coming for a number of events, which included Sundays, and that these were particularly focused on evangelism so don't invite your non-Christian friends. You see the church knew that normally if I was speaking it was so you could invite your friends who weren't Christians. They had changed the default setting over a number of years. The funny thing is that still people did invite their friends! Why? They had a new default setting; they couldn't not do it, it's what they did!

Doors and Streets

Have you ever done door-to-door work and as you approached a house found yourself praying that they wouldn't be in? It's so scary, isn't it? I should love it more than anyone as it is how my family became Christians.

When I first trained in evangelism, the streets would form the daily rhythm of my ministry. I had some amazing conversations with people and I have to say I owe my communication skills to learning how to hold a crowd for ten minutes as I presented the gospel with my sketch-board. For those who haven't seen it, it's basically a more conversational and visual way to preach using a lettering technique called ladder lettering where you draw several ladders on your board, which attracts the crowd, and then with flicks of your paintbrush you fill in the ladders to reveal words.

At the beginning of the chapter I listed three areas for evangelism and so I want to briefly touch on the second one here. It's been a long time since I did street and door evangelism, and so there will be many people better equipped than I to teach on this. However, I've seen enough and done enough to be able to share a bit of thinking here.

Day after day, in the temple courts and from house to house,
they never stopped teaching and proclaiming the good news that
Jesus is the Messiah. (Acts 5:42)

I love the fact that just after the Holy Spirit fell on the day of Pentecost, with the promise of "you will be my witnesses" being fulfilled, they immediately set about doing the witnessing. I've heard it said that we are meant to "be witnesses" and actually I agree but the result of the day of Pentecost was that they got busy "doing witnessing".

Let me say two things:

1. **It was day after day:** there was an intentional rhythm in place which was all about relational evangelism and proclamation evangelism. They weren't just doing it at their festivals in an ad-hoc, hit-and-run way; it was daily and consistent.

2. **Temple courts and homes:** it was public and it was private. This was in the Gentile courts which were very much seen as the place good for evangelism as there were public assemblies – particularly of Gentiles. It wasn't inside the temple building, it was out where many would be free to walk and so they took full advantage. Not only were they seeing the public opportunity of a crowd but also the private opportunity of the individual, and so they would go from home to home with this renewed passion, even though they would be under fire!

I totally believe in door-to-door evangelism and open-air evangelism but I believe, as I do with all our outreach, it has to be relational to be most fruitful. It wasn't just one night in June and that was it; when I became a Christian Brian and Godfrey and a few others visited us over a period of about six weeks, and then we went to the church.

I want to suggest that most of our door-to-door evangelism and street work should sit in the Healthy Maybe. As you begin to build relationally, you see the Little Yes build and you can always then hit the seasons and rhythms of the year to present the Big Yes. Many of the HOPE resources would work brilliantly on the doors and streets. As you get amongst the Healthy Maybe people you will begin to see where God is at work and then you can journey with them relationally, connecting them into the

Big Yes, Little Yes, Healthy Maybe events you have bubbling along in your church.

Below is a survey I have created and used to good effect. It's a starter to get you doing some Healthy Maybe stuff on the doors and streets. Why not start doing this in your community.

Good, Bad or Far Worse Survey

How good do you think the world is?

Good   Bad   Far worse

How good do you think the future is?

Good   Bad   Far worse

How good do you think your life is?

Good   Bad   Far worse

How good do you think you are?

Good   Bad   Far worse

How good an answer do you think religion is?

Good   Bad   Far worse

How good an answer do you think God is?

Good   Bad   Far worse

I would encourage you to link all that you do wherever possible to a key area of influence e.g. where you do your community engagement. I say this because I have seen churches who are nowhere near their city centre doing outreach there. I am not sure this is the best use of time or a good way of building relationally.

In the next chapter we will begin to look at community engagement and Big Yes, Little Yes, Healthy Maybe. We can begin to create a really good framework for all our outreach as we pick up on the third area of the three main ways a church can engage people with the gospel in their outreach.

#WeCan'tCreateSoulsButWeCanCreateJourney

Journey

Ashamed of who he had become, Rich Old was challenged to have a proper look at the Christian faith, and when he did he realised all his preconceived ideas about it were far from the truth of what it actually was.

They say life begins at forty, and for me that couldn't be more true! Shortly after my fortieth birthday, I'd flown a microlight, learned to ride a motorbike and quit an addiction I'd had for more than twenty years. None of these were things I'd predicted less than six months earlier and frankly they all came as a bit of a surprise. However, by far the biggest surprise and complete life-transformation took place when I discovered faith and when I met my Lord and saviour, Jesus Christ. Nobody saw that one coming, least of all me!

Faith played absolutely no part in the first forty years of my life whatsoever. My upbringing was very non-Christian: none of my family are religious and of all my friends, only one believed in God. So, religion was not something I could relate to or understand. I'd had decent and supportive parents but a few wrong turns led me to a life of false happiness, fake contentment and where I would become my own worst critic and enemy.

I wasn't proud of the lifestyle I was leading or many of the things I'd done. I've made plenty of bad choices, mixed with a few 'unsavoury' and even toxic people and got into some unpleasant situations along the way. I'd walked down the corridors of life looking for happiness, love, purpose and fulfilment ... but mainly found dead ends, false hope and mistrust.

I was ashamed of who I'd become and had developed a strong dislike of myself. To attempt to cope with life, I'd built a thick layer of armour to deal with the failings, guilt and bitterness that lay on my shoulders. I never once considered sharing or off-loading the burden: it was my problem and my fault, so I had to live with it. I was beyond redemption. There was nothing or nobody that could take that away. Even if there was a God, why would he help me?

Despite the baggage I was carrying, I somehow managed to marry Marie, the one person I'd known for years who knew Jesus. We now have two wonderful kids and between them, my family kept my head just above water ... but my "armour" was beginning to flake away and the "act" of being happy was becoming harder to maintain. My confidence and self-esteem had long gone and a deep depression had crept up on me and taken hold. I'd made my bed too small to lie in and it was getting very uncomfortable!

By the end of 2016 life had become particularly stressful.

The unshakeable dark clouds had descended and choked any remaining hope. I was lost and unable to cope, my marriage was put to the test and there was simply no more space under the carpet to sweep my issues. My "floor" had become too bumpy and I suffered a major breakdown. When I realised that I was no longer able to be the "rock" to my wife or family, I knew I'd reached my lowest point – destroyed. I wanted to hide away from everything and everyone.

I knew the lifestyle I'd led had to change and I slowly began to piece together the jigsaw that lay in front of me. I wasn't even sure what the final picture looked like but I soon realised that some of the pieces were missing. There was a hole in my heart but I had no idea how to fill it.

My wife Marie had begun to attend Redeemer King Church in Chesterfield on a regular basis which I didn't mind at all. She'd suggested that I join her on several occasions but I'd been dismissive. While I respected Marie's faith and knew that knowing God brought comfort to many people, it couldn't ever be for me. However, I needed to be with my family, so one Sunday I decided to go to church. I didn't know what to expect, I just wanted to support Marie.

I didn't pay much attention to the sermon and if anyone talked to me afterwards I'd tell folks that Christianity wasn't for me. Even if I was interested, I didn't deserve to be involved. But despite my declaration, and to my surprise, I was still welcomed and somehow left feeling more peaceful than when I arrived.

I went to Redeemer King a few more times with the same intentions but each time left feeling better than when I arrived. There was no pressure from anybody to investigate this thing called faith, just gentle words of encouragement and an overwhelming acceptance of who I was – something I couldn't even do for myself.

I didn't plan to be part of the church; this wasn't going to be my family. I didn't deserve that ... yet something about the people I met was different. A warmth, something welcoming and appealing. I couldn't put my finger on it but I now know that it was the Holy Spirit working within them. It gave me a sceptical curiosity but I knew it would be something I didn't deserve and could never have.

In February 2017 I agreed to attend an Alpha launch event at Redeemer King Church. When the evening came, Marie told me that she didn't really know what to expect but it could be a bit "sales-like". I distinctly remember chuntering about "not going to be buying anything" because I didn't really want to go. However, once I got there the people were once again welcoming with a kind of "light" shining from within. It made me think: are all these amazing people actually wrong, or could there be something in it?

A seed was planted that evening. Although I presumed that Jesus wouldn't want a relationship with me, perhaps I could understand a bit more about my wife's faith and the Christians I'd met in recent weeks – after all, I'd met a few and none turned out to be Ned Flanders (one of my many misconceptions about churchgoers). I left the Alpha launch night with a voice reverberating around my head: "Go and take a proper look. There's nothing to lose but potentially everything to gain!" (These were the words of Mark Greenwood, the Alpha launch speaker for the night.) Had I ever looked properly? No.

After much deliberation and several lengthy chats, I signed up to the Alpha course. I'd heard some intriguing testimonies and I wanted to understand more about faith in other people – and I still had "Go take a proper look" echoing around my head. I'd leave my cynical side at home and go to Alpha with an open mind to learn about other people's faith, but also to dismiss this whole Jesus thing for myself. I wasn't going to give this Jesus a chance to reject me, so I took that decision away from everybody else and excluded myself. At least it would be an informed decision. Of course, I'd be respectful because I'd been treated well and didn't want to waste anyone's time. I at least owed that to Dan (the host pastor who would become a good friend).

Once the Alpha course began it immediately felt like a comfortable, open and "safe" environment in which to listen, learn and ask questions. I soon realised that the conversation with Christians and the other non-Christian was an invaluable part of exploring. By week three I knew that the life, death and resurrection of Jesus were true! What a thing to discover; I'd been wrong for all these years! The people I'd met through church were right all along! I felt overwhelmingly happy for them but also sad that I was beyond redemption – it could have been nice but I was convinced

that Jesus would reject me, so there was no point in hoping for anything different. My view of Christians would never be the same again. The evening ended too soon and, with mixed emotions, I offered Dan a lift home, secretly wanting the opportunity to talk more.

That night my life would change forever. Dan and I sat talking about Alpha and I gave a very small glimpse into my past and my burdens. There was no detail but what he said next was an impossible comment to make based on what I'd said. The words "Jesus forgives you but perhaps you need to forgive yourself" had me pinned back in the chair in which I sat. I couldn't speak. I couldn't move. I couldn't understand how Dan had said something that I'd unknowingly been longing to hear for a very long time. I wanted to laugh and cry at the same time but couldn't even make a sound.

When I was eventually able to move again, I'd become a different person. All my burdens had evaporated; the weight on my shoulders was gone. Just gone! I still couldn't find any words. I didn't understand what had just happened but I was completely blown away. That night Jesus had met with me and I felt his overwhelming love for the very first time. I'd been saved from myself: my chains were broken and I'd been set free. I received forgiveness, a new lens through which to view life and the ice-cube in my heart had melted away. I'd reached out for the very first time to find Jesus had been there all along. This was not at all what I expected when I signed up for Alpha, but that night I got home, dropped to my knees and said my first prayer.

I awoke the next morning wondering if it had all been a dream but the feelings from the night before were still there. I'd also rediscovered the unfamiliar feeling of hope, joy and clearer skies ahead. The long battle I'd been fighting had already been won. This was no dream – it was indescribably better! I'd been completely forgiven.

On Tuesday 14th March 2017 I met with Dan and told him that I wanted to be all in for Christ. I had never been so certain about anything in my life and I knew it was the best decision I'd ever make (just as Dan had told me). It turned out that signing up to the Alpha course would become more life-changing than I could ever have imagined!

In the days that followed, my wife had to keep checking she had the right husband. Little did I know that these events had been an answer to years of prayer for her. At last I'd found faith and we could walk on the same path together. I was full of the Holy Spirit, full of love, hope, peace and joy. I hardly recognised myself ... or the things I was saying and doing.

I'd spent my whole adult life avoiding the spotlight and avoiding interaction with people, yet just days after going all-in for Jesus I found myself nervously standing in front of my Redeemer King family at the Easter Sunday service. At such a significant event in the Christian calendar I was gifted with the enormous privilege of publicly declaring my faith and telling my own story of re-birth. I'd finally arrived at home and in July 2017 was baptised by Dan and Beechy, two inspiring people I've come to know as friends.

So here I am, walking with Jesus and discovering things about myself that I didn't know were in me! I've been given a gift to encourage others and love to see people succeed. I've discovered that I actually quite like meeting new people, especially welcoming them into a church-related environment if they are unfamiliar. I find myself getting really excited when presented with an opportunity to speak about Jesus – some even say there is an evangelist in me!

Of course, none of this would have happened without Alpha giving me the opportunity to "take a proper look"; it was truly the start line for my life being completely transformed – I'm so happy that I took the time! I have a love and passion for the Alpha course and prayed for the Lord to use me in some way with the next event. Sure enough God responded by letting me speak at the 2018 Redeemer King Alpha launch night and allowing me to help out over the twelve-week course. It was a privilege to see three amazing people come to Christ and get baptised soon after! I've also recently begun a new Alpha course with more incredible people and am leading a small group table – a minor achievement for some but a huge step for me!

Meeting Jesus has been an adventure full of discovery and surprises and I can't wait to see where he leads me next. I've still got a long journey to become the man I want to be but, with his help and guidance, I've left the man I was a long way behind! I've been blessed with new hope, a reignited love for life, an amazing church family and a refreshed marriage, and it's all down to the love of Jesus, my saviour who set me free.

7
Using BYLYHM in Community Engagement

"It's good to see some of our food bank people at the Christmas event this evening" (Northumberland)

"Our divorce recovery workshop loved it this evening" (Warwickshire)

One of my favourite organisations is CAP (Christians Against Poverty). This isn't just because it started in Bradford where I grew up and lived until about the age of twenty-five, but rather the commitment they have to releasing someone of their spiritual as well as financial debts. I love it! At its heart is to love people. They are a words-and-deeds movement.

Probably one of the most used quotes when thinking about demonstrating the gospel through actions is attributed to Saint Francis of Assisi even though we don't really know whether he actually said it! "Preach the gospel at all times. When necessary, use words."

The quote kind of polarises people a bit. I have known some of my friends in the church tell me it's a compromise and some tell me it's wisdom! If we assume he did say it, we ought to find out a bit more about him so we can understand the context. Saint Francis was committed to being a model of what it meant be a follower of Christ. He was a creative and visual preacher both in the open air as well as the church. He would have incredible prose as well as a more fun side to his speaking.

Jamie Arpin-Ricci is the author of *Vulnerable Faith* and *The Cost of Community*. He wrote a great article called "Preach the Gospel at All Times?" In it he writes:

> *St Francis never sought to elevate action over speaking in the task of bringing the Gospel, but neither did he believe that Gospel was only a message to be communicated. Francis recognised that the Gospel was all consuming, the work of God to restore all of Creation unto himself for his glory. He embraced the truth that the authority of the Gospel he proclaimed with his mouth was given authority by the nature and character of the life he led. And in the same way, he knew that, in spite of his own failings (and that of other Christians), the proclaimed message of hope and love would find fertile soil in the hearts of others, and so that Gospel must be proclaimed.*[13]

You see far from being a compromise, this, for me, is exactly what community engagement and social action should be. I believe as we do community engagement we should keep the gospel in words in one lens and the gospel in deeds in the other lens: those are the glasses through which we should look.

Over the thirty-one years I have been in full-time evangelism, I've noticed a pendulum swing. When I first started out proclamation evangelism was high on the agenda. Then the conversation swung to whether there was any real need to make appeals anymore and it wasn't long after that the conversation became about whether we really need to even share or preach the gospel. I remember at the time expressing to my friend (a fellow evangelist) that we were in danger of losing the belief in the power of preaching. Don't get me wrong, I believe it was a shift that was needed but not at the expense of remaining verbally silent. For me evangelism must be in words and deeds and all of this through and in the power of the Spirit.

I am glad to say, however, that I believe we have come to a more balanced place and, by and large, we know that we need both. We have looked at Big Yes, Little Yes, Healthy Maybe in the context of local church evangelism and in the next chapters we will look at it in the context of church planting, preaching and personal evangelism, but is it possible to connect all this to community engagement and social action? I say yes (and that's a Big Yes!). You see this is no new tension. You can go back to St Francis and see that he, too, carried the same tension and passion.

> **Evangelism must be in words and deeds and all of this through and in the power of the Spirit.**

Historically, many churches on the more conservative/evangelical end of the church haven't really focused a lot on social action and caring for those who live in the margins. We have often relegated it to being of secondary importance at best and left it to the more liberal end of the church and yet we have often told this story in our Sunday schools:

> *On one occasion an expert in the law stood up to test Jesus. "Teacher," he asked, "what must I do to inherit eternal life?"*
>
> *"What is written in the Law?" Jesus replied. "How do you read it?"*
>
> *He answered, "'Love the Lord your God with all your heart and with all your soul and with all your strength and with all your mind' and*

'Love your neighbour as yourself.'"

"You have answered correctly," Jesus said. "Do this and you will live." But he wanted to justify himself, so he asked Jesus, "And who is my neighbour?"

In reply Jesus said, "A man was going down from Jerusalem to Jericho when he was attacked by robbers. They stripped him of his clothes, beat him and went away, leaving him half-dead. A priest happened to be going down the same road, and when he saw the man, he passed by on the other side. So too, a Levite, when he came to the place and saw him, passed by on the other side. But a Samaritan, as he travelled, came where the man was; and when he saw him, he took pity on him. He went to him and bandaged his wounds, pouring on oil and wine. Then he put the man on his own donkey, brought him to an inn, and took care of him. The next day he took out two denarii and gave them to the innkeeper. 'Look after him,' he said, 'and when I return, I will reimburse you for any extra expense you may have.' Which of these three do you think was a neighbour to the man who fell into the hands of robbers?" The expert in the law replied, "The one who had mercy on him." Jesus told him, "Go and do likewise." (Luke 10:25–37)

In Acts 10:37–38 Luke says, "You know what has happened throughout the province of Judea, beginning in Galilee after the baptism that John preached – how God anointed Jesus of Nazareth with the Holy Spirit and power, and how he went around doing good and healing all who were under the power of the devil, because God was with him."

Quite apart from that the fact Jesus did lots of miracles, Luke sees fit to draw our attention to the truth that Jesus went around doing good! This was an outcome of "God anointed Jesus of Nazareth with the Holy Spirit". An example of this was when he fed the 5000 and then spoke to them. Again Jesus placed a massive emphasis on "whatever you did for the least of these, you did for me", referencing, of course, giving cups of water to the thirsty and clothing the naked in his name.

Do it Because You Care

My concerns are we can do this purely as a means to preach, but actually we should do it because we care. I have to say I am not keen on the phrase "before we feed them spiritually we should feed them physically to earn the right". For me Jesus has commanded us and given us the authority to preach and to care. We do it because we love God and loving God must be accompanied by loving our neighbour as we have already seen in the Good Samaritan. Feed the poor and clothe the naked because it's the right thing to do and it's the Jesus thing to do. Let's feed the stomach and the soul!

Tell the Better Story

My friend often says, "People won't care what you know until they know that you care." We do need "what we know" to be connected with the care we show. I've come across some brilliant outreach that churches are doing but some of the beneficiaries of those projects didn't know that they were anything to do with the church that was running them, they simply happened in the church building. This doesn't feel right to me; we need to have a holistic approach to our community engagement and social action i.e. spiritual as well as physical and emotional. In truth we are doing them a disservice by not connecting it to the gospel in words.

We have an amazing opportunity to show people we care. As Christians we are often known by what we are against, but imagine being known by what we are for. Let's tell the better story and sometimes the best way of doing this is by being kind in our communities. As we do this we change the perceptions that many have of the Christian faith, creating a whole lot of Healthy Maybe connections; some will definitely become Little Yes people and later become Big Yes people.

The Healthy Maybe

I believe, from a missional perspective, our community engagement and social action needs to sit in the Healthy Maybe. There is no greater way to raise the Healthy Maybe in a community than these amazing projects. This has a geographical impact (how people feel about the church in their area), a theological impact (how people feel about Christianity) and a personal impact (how they feel about the Christian they know/are acquainted with). This is such a great way to get a relational build in your community and you get to see where God is at move in people's lives. I often talk about community engagement to gospel engagement and this is so we avoid two extremes that are unhelpful. We have already talked about the one extreme – doing it so we can preach – but the other extreme we must avoid is simply showing love to people but not accompanying it with words. Either is not really a true reflection of the mission of God.

Discipleship Matters

It's worth saying briefly here that as we engage with some of the more marginalised in society, it brings with it its challenges. Discipling people from the poor and needy in society will look different from how we make disciples of others. This is where the individual pathway and not just collective programme are relevant in terms of making disciples.

Our world is getting increasingly messier and it shows no signs of getting better. Increasingly people will challenge our theology by their life choices but let's treat them with dignity and love whilst holding onto truth. I am forever grabbed by this verse that we so often partially quote:

> *The Word became flesh and made his dwelling among us. We have seen his glory, the glory of the one and only Son, who came from the Father, full of grace and truth. (John 1:14)*

Notice it doesn't say "truth and grace", which so often can be the approach we use, but rather let us be "full of grace and truth" because that is how Jesus arrived into our mess.

Of course the other side of this is that existing Christians have a way of being missionally operational as they feel able to serve through their passion. This is a great cause and a cause is something we all need.

The Gospel and Social Engagement

My very good friend Mike Royal was the first ever chair of my evangelistic ministry. He is someone who understands community engagement and gospel engagement and how they fuse together. Mike is the Co Chief Executive of the Cinnamon Network. He is the former National Director and national pioneer of Transforming Lives for Good (TLG). He is also a mental health chaplain in a medium secure context, with an academic background in urban planning and black theology. Living in Birmingham UK, he is a Pentecostal Bishop and has been in pastoral ministry for over twenty-five years. He writes ...

MIKE ROYAL

The dichotomy between evangelism and social action in the church is an historic tale of missed opportunities. In his book *Whatever Happened to Evangelical Social Action*, Bill Johnson, writing from a Western perspective, outlines the polemic between liberal and the fundamentalist wings of the church. Evangelical churches have historically taken a personal approach to solving problems. The solution for the evangelical church has been to deal with the problem of personal sin in the individual. Liberal churches, on the other hand, have taken a societal position, seeking to reform society's structures. The solution for the liberal church has been to deal with the problem of what I am going to call "structural sin" in wider society.

The Social Reformers

The roots of the liberal fundamentalist conflict can actually be traced right back to the reformation. Yet history tells us that the people who have made their mark on church history in the West over the last 200 years have been those who have adopted a "both, and" approach to tackling personal and structural sin. Think of William Wilberforce, appealing to both the hearts of men and to society as he worked towards the passing of the act to abolish the slave trade in 1807. William Booth, arguably the founder of social services as we know it before any local government, had a word-and-deed approach in the late nineteenth century through his work with the Salvation Army. Revd Dr Martin Luther King Jr again appealed both to the hearts of people as well as challenging the oppressive structures, in tackling the scourge of racial segregation in 1950s and 1960s America.

The Church and Social Provision

In Great Britain, the nineteenth century saw many of the schools, hospitals and social services provision being pioneered by Christian leaders. In the twentieth century these services were "mainstreamed" by government with the establishment and development of the welfare state, particularly in the inter-war period. In the twenty-first century we have seen a distrust of the state developing and a rolling back of public service. While this should be lamented, it has also been an opportunity for the church to recognise and seek to address the gaps in social service provision.

My experience of pioneering Transforming Lives for Good alternative education provision schools in partnership with churches and leading one of the first Ascension Trust Street Pastors teams in north Birmingham between 2004 and 2009, has helped shape my perspective. What we *do* as a church has a huge impact on how people receive what we *say* as a church. How does our social action open up the opportunity to share our faith with credibility? How do we share the gospel in a way that leads us to follow it up with practical social action?

Creating Proximity

The first thing social action does is to create proximity between the church and the community.

The Eden Project movement, led by The Message Trust, has emphasised it's only as the church "moves into the neighbourhood" that it can really touch the lives of people in disadvantaged communities. The recent Estates Movement, led by Anglican bishop Philip North, is encouraging the pioneering of churches on Britain's so called "left behind" estates in outer-city communities. Being a street pastor in Aston, Lozells and Handsworth enabled me to more fully understand what was going on in the community, how to respond to people's individual holistic needs, and how to advise civic agencies to respond in a practical way. It gave me an awareness of the issues on the ground and a feel for how the church could respond relevantly.

Developing Relationships

The second thing social action does for the church is to aid it in developing relationships with everyday people. Cinnamon Network is all about helping churches with gospel-centred community engagement. Cinnamon has over thirty projects run by organisations who have committed to partner with the local church. Who Let the Dads Out?, pioneered by Mark Chester and Tony Sharp, is a parent-and-toddler group for dads. Box Up Crime, pioneered by Stephen Addison, supports churches to set up non-contact boxing clubs for disengaged young people. Parish Nursing, pioneered by Helen Wordsworth, puts a nurse in a local church to serve those in the church and in the local community.

What do all these projects have in common? Essentially they are about building relationships through meeting people at the point of their need. It's not about projects being done *to* people; it's about projects being a practical means to help the church engage *with* people.

Offering Sanctuary

I believe a community of believers can be a place of sanctuary. Bill Hybels famously said, "The local church is the hope of the world." In Birmingham we have recently seen the development of "Places of Welcome" which have been developed by Thrive Together Birmingham, the Church Urban

Fund Joint Venture. Places of Welcome are essentially churches that choose to open their doors and offer a welcome, friendship, support and a listening ear to everyone in the community.

Theologian Leslie Newbiggin put it like this: "I have come to feel that the primary reality of which to take into account in seeking impact on public life, is a Christian congregation ... How is it possible that the gospel should be credible? ... I am suggesting the only answer, the only hermeneutic of the gospel [the best interpretation of the gospel], is a congregation of men and women who believe it and live by it." All of our social action, all of our community project work is futile unless it is rooted in a local congregation. That's why the Cinnamon Network is only interested in working through the local church.

Taking Opportunities

The church must resist the accusations of those who say we are "proselytising". What many agencies are asking the church to do is to bring our energy to the table but leave the source of that energy, Jesus, at the door. Not me! We must bring our whole selves to the public square as ministers of the gospel. Sometimes as a church minister I find it helpful to wear my clerical collar when attending meetings with statutory agencies, so they know exactly who I am and what I represent.

Social action projects often touch people at the point of their need. People often come to faith at a point of crisis in their lives. I did! The mercy ministries that maximise that opportunity will be those who are most effective at bringing personal transformation and a well of practical help.

Churches Bringing Transformation

I saw Yardley Wood Baptist Church take a huge step and partner with Transforming Lives for Good and run an alternative education centre in south Birmingham for disengaged young people at risk of exclusion from school. I saw that church changed from a struggling outer-city church, to a community church accessed by so many people in the locality. It was as if they sowed in one place and reaped in many places. There is something fruitful that happens when the church opens its doors to the community.

I love the work of Christians Against Poverty, founded by John Kirkby, who do all their debt counselling work through the local church. They will offer to pray with people, they will share their faith with people, while they are supporting people exiting a life of debt. They will celebrate at their head office when someone comes to faith through the work of their local church partners. I wish every organisation was as intentional about the gospel and social action going hand in glove as CAP.

My final example is one from my own local church. The North Birmingham TLG alternative education centre had a rising rap artist attending the centre. Sadly he died in a drug-fuelled car accident with his uncle. The staff at the centre visited, supported and even arranged the funeral for the family which hundreds of young people attended. He had quite a music following. The circumstances of his death led to division in the family and mum having to move away. She moved from north Birmingham to south Birmingham to live a few doors down from a lady she had never met but who attended my church. This lady befriended her, led her to faith and brought her to church. I arrived one Sunday morning to find this mother who I had supported 18 months before, standing before me excited about her newfound faith in Jesus. That's what God does when the church rolls up its sleeves and helps the last, the least and the lost!

Social Action and Church Growth

In conclusion, I recently attended the launch of the Grace Project by Theos and the Church Urban Fund at Lambeth Palace with Archbishop Justin Welby. The project is researching the relationship between social action, church growth and discipleship. What a great research subject area. What a great conversation. Watch this space ...

Six Models for Community Engagement

I detail here six distinct stand-alone models for community engagement. These are not exhaustive and can be fused together for bigger impact. I simply list them this way to enable buy-in for churches that could feel a bit overawed by the task at hand.

1. Multi projects

Run by your church and connecting to each other i.e. people who need food probably need financial management help, etc., the aim being that we don't just meet a single need but we seek to meet the many needs.

2. Community assisted

You ask your community to help you meet the needs of the community. This is particularly powerful as the people in your community see love in action as they help you. There are many stories of people who have come to faith as they got engaged in this. There was a man at a church I was speaking at a number of years ago who was an atheist but heard about what they were doing in the community. He asked the minister if he could get involved (telling him that he was an atheist). Through this he came to faith.

3. Where there's a crowd there's a Christian

The aim here is that as opposed to starting up lots of projects from the church where maybe people and finances are stretched, the local church would identify secular community projects that a member or members of that church can get involved with and seek to influence by simply being present.

4. Council partnership

Contact the council and find out what the needs are and then offer to set up projects that meet the target needs of the council. Funding is available then because it meets the criteria for the council. Better to know what the genuine needs are than invest where we don't know for definite.

5. Joint churches

Work with churches across your town, city or area to support community projects e.g. Foodbank, CAP, Street Angels, TLG, Intentional Health, etc. This is great from a kingdom perspective as it shows the church united and not divided. Churches can pool people, buildings and financial resources. There is potential for expertise to exist in other churches that isn't in your own.

6. Planting churches

I will pick up on this in greater detail later but just to put a marker down here: a church or individual identifies an area where they feel they should plant. This model of planting would be by means of identifying the social needs in that area and, rather than simply starting a church, they start a community engagement project. In due course they plant a church that may become a traditional model or may simply be a fresh expression or home-based church. Expecting people in socially deprived areas to travel to a church building nowhere near where they live can often present an unnecessary barrier.

Organisations

Listed below are a few organisations doing some great work helping churches with their community engagement. They have some incredible expertise and proven track records. Why not make contact with them and see if they can help you. These organisations are led by people I have known and trusted for many years.

- **Cinnamon network: cinnammonnetwork.org.uk**

  Cinnamon Network aims to make it as easy as possible for local churches to transform their communities by reaching out and building life-giving relationships with those in greatest need.

• **Future Kraft: www.futurekraft.org**

Providing local organisations with the tools, experience and practical skills they need to develop sustainable projects.

• **ROC (Redeeming Our Communities): www.rocuk.com**

ROC's main aim is to bring about community transformation by creating strategic partnerships between statutory agencies, voluntary groups and churches. These partnerships form new volunteer-led projects that address a variety of social needs.

#WeCan'tCreateSoulsButWeCanCreateJourney

Journey

Having only a few memories of his childhood and enduring some of life's big challenges, Ron eventually signed up to the police where he witnessed things he never expected. Feeling loved and wanted by a church he started attending, Ron is now on his way back to God.

I was born into a family with a strict and ritualistic religion. I only have two recollections as an infant: sitting in assembly listening to a nun play the violin; and being at home when a large gate fell on me as I closed it. I sustained a head injury requiring a few days in hospital. It appeared that someone had loosened the top hinge.

My father joined the army and we moved to Germany. Our parents treated us badly and I remember being beaten with a large plastic tennis racquet and being slapped about the face and head. I remember having to empty buckets of faeces and urine. I only had one friend whose name was Ronnie; I just didn't know how to socialise. I always seemed to be in conflict with my siblings. We were told that we were bad children and that we weren't going to heaven. We had to give love but it didn't seem to be returned by our parents. I vaguely remember Sunday school; I thought God was good, that he loved us and he would protect us, but where was he? Maybe I was bad.

We returned to the UK where the beatings with the racquet stopped but the slaps continued. Because I'd attended seven different schools I was behind with my education but I did manage to catch up and get my qualifications. Because of our religion we were segregated to a classroom during school assembly. I later decided to join the main assembly which my parents were not happy about. By now I really didn't want to be with my family. I had no love for them.

I joined the police as a cadet when I was sixteen. I couldn't wait to leave home. How was it possible that I felt homesick? Homesick for what? I was confused. I found it very hard but I managed to get through. I still struggled to make friends but I did meet some good people.

I joined the regular police force and was posted to quite a hard town, which I wasn't really prepared for, but after my two-year probationary period my appointment as constable was confirmed. I married but we separated after about a year as I just didn't have the necessary skills to cope with married life. It was hard but I concentrated on my duties. My wife and I later reconciled and we eventually had a daughter. I found being a father hard but I tried my best.

It was decided that we should move to another station so that we could start anew. We moved to a small rural town, very different from where I had originally been stationed. I felt that life was starting to show some promise.

I was on duty one evening when a garbled message came through that an officer in a nearby town needed urgent assistance. I sped to his assistance, along with some other officers, but it was too late. He was lying on the pavement being tended to by an ambulance man but died at the scene of his injuries. I wanted to react like a normal person would but I knew I had to stay focused. There was no counselling in those days; the senior officers only wanted to know where we had been when the officer had been killed. It gave the impression that somehow we had failed him. I was in another town, for goodness' sake. It changed me. We were supposed to be the good guys, we were young and superhuman. We were supposed to get the bad guys, but the bad guys had won. Where was God to protect us? This is where the relationship between me and God ended. It was just me against the rest of the world. I trusted no-one. No-one loved me.

I moved to several other stations but all I saw was the evil in the world. I just plodded on feeling that I wasn't going to make a difference. The bad guys always seemed to win. It was a dark time. But whilst at a rural station I had the privilege to meet and tutor a young woman. She had a very strong faith in God which I have to say I didn't understand. To this day I bitterly regret deriding her faith. Surprisingly she allowed me to become a friend.

My wife and I divorced after sixteen years of marriage, most likely due to the stresses and strains of police life. We now had two daughters and I regret the effect it had on all of us. I later retired from the police due to ill health and had time to reflect on my life; this seemed to have a calming effect. I often wondered why our parents had treated us like they had; perhaps they had been treated badly when they were young.

I met and married the most wonderful woman. I learned to understand that there were good and happy families. It was hard at first as I thought that family life was what I had previously experienced. I started to trust again. The young lady that I had tutored years before invited me to her church. I was in a lot of physical pain at that time due to an injury incurred at work so found it difficult to absorb what was going on. I do know that I was made very welcome. By this time I had four wonderful grandchildren. I loved them and they loved me. With children their love is unconditional. I think they gave me more than I gave to them and I realised that what had happened to me was life.

Once I was able to cope with the physical pain I again visited the church. I was made to feel very wanted. People were very welcoming, kind and considerate, and despite whatever difficulties they had, their faith in God was very strong. I realised that my faith had not ended but had stalled. It was time to let God back into my life. Despite what has happened to me I believe God gave me the strength to get to where I am now.

I am a survivor not a victim.

8

Using BYLYHM in Church Planting

ave you ever thought about this? Every church in the United Kingdom was once a church plant!

Even as I write that it seems obvious. There seems to be many national conversations going on right now and church planting is one of them. Big Yes, Little Yes, Healthy Maybe has an impact on church planting.

It would be true to say that I have spoken in many church plants down through the years and I have also advised church leaders on evangelism as they felt God was nudging them to plant a church. Some of my friends have planted churches and I have listened pastorally as they have been through the hard times that inevitably happen with any pioneer work. The truth is, I could have a reasonable go at writing this chapter and I am sure it would be helpful but I decided not to! Why? Because the truth is, outside of the aforementioned, I have not been actively involved in church planting, nor have I read much around the subject.

Thankfully I work with a great man and long-term friend, Revd Gary Gibbs, who not only heads up church planting for Elim Pentecostal Church, he also has great insight into the area and has been involved in planting a church. Gary also understands the Big Yes, Little Yes, Healthy Maybe philosophy, and believes in it, so he is best placed to write this chapter. I asked and he said yes so my thanks to Gary.

GARY GIBBS

What's so difficult about planting a new church? Raise a pot of money, find a venue, recruit a worship band, a few "meeters and greeters", and plaster the town with leaflets and advertisements. Hey presto! At your first service you'll have a whole bunch of people turn up. And, most probably, they will nearly all be Christians already.

It's possible to plant a religious service into an area rather than planting a church. In fact, even the term "church planting" is not that helpful these days; rather, we should be trying to plant the gospel into a community and, as people eventually begin to respond with a Big Yes to Jesus, we gather them together and we have church!

Before I go any further, let me qualify something. It is totally possible to begin a new church by starting an attractive service in a community. This can work as long as you have a bunch of dedicated Jesus followers who live there and who are engaged with neighbours, work colleagues, family members, friends who also live there. In fact, if your team have been sharing about Jesus with their contacts for a good length of time before a church plant was even considered and they have communicated in an effective manner, you may find early on that there are people who are ready to say the Big Yes once given the opportunity.

The challenge really kicks in once you have harvested the "low hanging fruit". How do you reach those who are far away from God?

First: Healthy Maybe

I was involved with a church plant where the first activity we did was to launch a Kids' Club. The idea was that the primary-aged children from our team members would bring along their friends. There would be lots of fun and activities but also an opportunity to learn about Jesus, the gospel and to make decisions to follow him.

It was a disaster.

When the kids went home and explained to their sophisticated upper-middle-class parents what had happened, the parents concluded that we were a cult that was after their children. The Kids' Club shut down very quickly. It took a few years to re-establish trust and credibility in the neighbourhood.

Here, then, is a suggested guide to the steps involved in planting the gospel, and then a church, in a place.

1. Pray!

In Matthew 9 Jesus tells his disciples that there are masses of people without God (the harvest) and that there are few believers reaching them. So, what to do? The very first thing, says Jesus, is to ask the Father to send out workers into the harvest fields. In other words, they should PRAY!

There is an acronym which is sometimes used: P.U.S.H. which stands for "Pray Until Something Happens!" This is the foundation to any success in evangelism. Notice that Jesus specifically instructs the disciples to pray for other team members rather than to intercede for lost people. It's not that praying for the salvation of others is wrong, but the more gospel workers we have, the merrier! And it's worth noting that as they prayed, they themselves were sent out (Matthew 10:5). We are often the answer to our own prayers!

Our prayer life, both individually and corporately, will be the lifeblood of our missional activity. God will change the atmosphere over a place when we pray. He will create the most amazing "coincidences". He will open doors for evangelistic opportunity. He will open hearts to the possibility of finding hope, meaning and purpose. He will intrigue people into wanting to find out more about him. He will eventually enable them to deliberately decide to follow Jesus. In other words, BYLYHM will happen, usually in the reverse order! HMLYBY!!

2. Think and act like a missionary

The best missionaries are those who are not only called by God to go but also work hard on prior planning and preparation. What does that look like if you are a missionary in the West?

Well, you will need to understand the culture of the place: what are their values? What is the history? What are the strongly held beliefs, preferences and/or prejudices? Where and how do people gather, and for what? Are there any peculiarities about how they use language? How and what do they celebrate? Who do they trust and why?

My wife and I planted on a social housing estate in the mid-1990s. At Christmas we invited all our neighbours to a "sherry and mince pie evening". Not one person showed up! We had totally missed it culturally! We now live in a village in a semi-rural location. Every Christmas our neighbours come around late morning to early afternoon. For what? Sherry, mince pies, coffee, etc. We learnt our lesson!

3. Find the Person(s) of Peace

This approach is taken from Jesus's instructions to the 70 before he sent them out in Luke 10.

There are particular people in a new community who God has prepared to welcome you and to facilitate you getting to know others in the area quite quickly. The person of peace is often someone of influence and well known by many. At the beginning, this person may not be a Christian, but they are open to you and the Good News you want to bring. Building a strong link here is super important. They may soon become a Little Yes person and move onto Big Yes ahead of many!

4. Become a Friend of Sinners!

Laurence Singlehurst, a writer, thinker and activist on all things missional, suggests that we need to ask ourselves, "How many hands are we holding?" In other words, how many meaningful friendships are we building in this community? Somewhere else he writes that the message we initially need to get across is that "God is good and we are OK!" This is, of course, all Healthy Maybe stuff!

Romans 8:29 tells us that we are on a journey even after our initial salvation "to be conformed to the image of his Son". In other words, to become more and more Christ like. The fact is that the more we become like Jesus, the more we will be friends, mates, buddies with those who don't yet know him.

Then: Little Yes, Big Yes

Once we have built relational bridges to those who are not following Jesus, we need as many entry points as possible for them to move on the journey towards the Lord.

Process evangelism courses such as Alpha are excellent ways to move people along. For some they act as a Little Yes and for many it brings them to the point of becoming fully fledged Jesus followers.

For other seekers, it could simply be in the ongoing relationship with one of God's people they come to the point of salvation. It's often at times of crisis that people open up to the need for salvation, but sometimes they just realise that their time has come and they need to surrender to King Jesus!

Again, it can happen in a Sunday service where the sense of God's presence overwhelms their limited resistance to him and/or the preaching of the Word does its work in their heart and life.

Afterwards: the Ongoing "Yeses"

The commission given to us is to make disciples (Matthew 28:18–20). What does that look like? Eugene Peterson described discipleship as "a long obedience in the same direction". One way of characterising true spiritual life is in terms of a series of yeses: even a Healthy Maybe could be a "micro yes". Certainly after we have said the initial Big Yes, God looks for us to consistently walk along a Yes path concerning his will and his ways.

I find it difficult to describe discipleship outside of a strong missional imperative: to authentically follow Jesus means we will go fishing!

And the end result of concerted fishing for people by the Jesus community must be that new Jesus communities are formed.

Why?

In his book *The Golden Circle*, the author Simon Sinek asks why it is that some organisations or companies are more influential or innovative than others. His conclusion is that they are the ones who do not simply deal with the "What?" and "How?" questions concerning what they are producing, but they ask the deeper question: "Why?"

When it comes to mission and church planting, we tend to jump straight to the What and How issues, the practicalities. But there is a deeper motivational factor which will keep us pressing forwards if we see it.

In John 20 the risen Lord Jesus appears to his disciples and, after calming them down, he tells them "As the Father has sent me, I am sending you." And with that he breathed on them and said, "Receive the Holy Spirit" (v. 21–22). This is what theologians call *missio Dei*, literally "the sending of God".

So why plant churches? Why reach out to those who don't know God? Often our default answer is that God has commanded us to do so in The Great Commission and of course this is true. But in his book, Ross Hastings suggests that John 20:21 is in fact The Greatest Commission.[14]

The essential nature of the God we love and follow is that he is a missional God who, out of his great love, is constantly sending: he sent his Son (John 3:16), he sent his Spirit (Acts 2) and now he sends his church to the world.

The "Why?" of outreach evangelism is that to be mission-shaped is to be godly! And by being this, we make Jesus very happy!

Let's say a Big Yes to God's mission so that others who don't know him will be able, ultimately, to say a Big Yes to the salvation he brings!

I'd like to finish this chapter with a very short paragraph. I believe the principles that Gary has addressed in this chapter would also work well in a re-plant. For the uninitiated, a re-plant is where a church has severely declined and needs new life breathing into it. There would obviously be some pastoral issues to deal with and tricky people to chat to but what better way to breathe new life into a church than turning it outward facing, and Big Yes, Little Yes, Healthy Maybe would certainly help with that. I've spoken at a number of replants down through the years and seen them grow well, even seeing original members come back. If fixed, the reasons people leave can be the doorway to them coming back.

#WeCan'tCreateSoulsButWeCanCreateJourney

Journey

Ready to listen and finally face the questions she had about life, Zoe Rayall had so far convinced herself that ignoring God was okay. But why miss out on all that God had for her when it was all that she really wanted?

I was brought up in a Christian family. My parents were heavily involved in the local church; Dad played the organ for weddings and services, ran the youth group and often preached. Growing up, church seemed like just another place I had to go, like school, and it certainly didn't seem to have any relevance for me. When I was twenty-three and had just graduated from university, my dad died from cancer. It was a tremendous shock for me, even though Mum and Dad had been told the chemotherapy had stopped working and he had chosen to be back at home. I remember a friend of mine at the time saying, "Didn't you talk to him about dying?" No, I didn't. I guess we were trying to remain positive and not even consider the possibility.

Dad dying gave me a valid reason to avoid facing the question of God. I mean how could God let my dad die – someone who had been such a big part of the church? I continued to live my life for the next fifteen years, moved out of home and eventually moved to another area of the country to further my career. Every so often, when I allowed myself to dream, I kept coming back to a deep feeling of wanting to work with and help people in some way, but this was always put on a back burner whilst life took over.

I met my husband in May 2011 (when I was thirty-eight) and we were engaged and married by May 2013. Six months later, to our surprise and excitement, we found out we were expecting our first baby. The pregnancy continued without any hiccups whilst I continued in my busy job working away four nights a week. My due date came and went and so I was booked in for an induction. Saturday morning we went to hospital and initial checks stopped my world. A heartbeat couldn't be found. We were sent home to return on the Monday, and our beautiful baby girl Grace was stillborn on August 4th 2014. I found out later that my mum was outside the door to my room on the ward praying for me, and the rest of her church and my sister back home, too. I can't explain it but at the time I felt an overwhelming sense of calm and peace after the birth, so I was able to focus on holding her and fully participating in those private, precious few hours.

I took my maternity leave, a year off work to be a parent, only

I wasn't able to take care of my baby. I started to volunteer in a local charity shop and at a drop-in centre for Mind, the mental health charity, whilst slowly allowing myself to adapt to a completely different pace of life. Five months later, after much encouragement not to put it off, I was once again pregnant and at the beginning of the long and daunting pregnancy journey all over again. It was whilst I was working at the charity shop that a customer asked me if my bump was my first child. I told her all about Grace and the conversation ended up with her inviting me to go to a local church with her. I started going Sunday mornings and would cry at every service. I confided in a few ladies about Grace and my fears for this pregnancy, and they prayed for me and my bump. Jack was born on 23rd September 2015 via caesarean section and, although he had a bit of a wobbly start, he was a healthy baby.

Mum's health had been deteriorating, but ever the trooper she did her best to hide it from family and friends. When Jack was seven months old Mum was admitted to the short-stay ward at hospital initially with dehydration; less than a week later she died peacefully, aged seventy-nine, with her three children at her side. At this time the church I was going to advertised a Reason to Believe course with Mark Greenwood. Okay, I thought, I'm ready to listen and finally face the questions I had about God that I had deliberately ignored. So I signed up for the evening meets. I was aware that my mum's parents had come to faith at the eleventh hour, so I had used that to convince myself that ignoring God was okay. Something that Mark said during his course hit home with me, "You can convert at the last minute but then you're missing out on knowing God, a Father who loves us and wants the best for us." Wow! A Father? I had forgotten what it felt like to have one.

But of course life took over and again God was put on the back burner. The three of us were now moving house and not just to any house, but back to my mum's house – the family home from when I was ten years old and had struggled to move out of after Dad died. So in February 2017 my husband, eighteen-month-old Jack and I moved back to the village where I grew up.

2017 was a tough year and put a real strain on our four-year marriage. Surrounded by constant reminders of my parents (it took us over a year to clear the house of belongings whilst living there), first-time parents to a "terrible two" toddler and visiting the village church graveyard where both my parents and daughter were buried, resulted in me snapping at my husband one minute and crying the next. I didn't want to go out and socialise and started asking myself the big questions: "What is life all about?" "Why are we here?" "What is the point?" In the end my husband suggested I talk to someone. I agreed but I knew that counselling couldn't answer all my questions. So I asked the vicar's wife whether there was an Alpha course that I could go to. She organised for the church's outreach worker to meet me and so for three months I had a weekly counselling session and a session at home with the outreach worker. This enabled me to work through the emotional rollercoaster I'd been on for the last three years at the same time as exploring the big questions about God. I agreed to look at some basic studies of the Bible at each session (using the *Live* book and DVD by Rebecca Manley Pippert), covering questions like "How do I know it's real?" and "Is it worth it?" At a church service in December 2017 there was a Christmas pamphlet which talked about life being like a puzzle and it made sense:

> *When we try to build our lives with ourselves in the centre, we inevitably fail. Like trying to put together a jigsaw by following the wrong picture, we find that it just doesn't work. And even if we muddle along and work out how to live and enjoy life, death still waits for us at the end.*

I was scared of death and dying and wanted all the parts of my life to make sense and actually mean something. And so I prayed the prayer in the pamphlet.

> *Lord Jesus Christ, thank you that you show the truth about God, the world and about my own life. I'm sorry for the way I have ignored you and pushed you out of your rightful place in the centre of my life. Thank you that you loved me enough to enter our world to show us the truth about God. Thank you that you loved me enough to die so I can find peace with God. Thank you that you rose again to give me new life forever.*

> *Please help me to receive these gifts this Christmas time. Amen.*

My sister told me recently that Mum and her friends had prayed that I would meet someone and my husband has been such a blessing from God. He has been extremely patient and supportive while I worked through some tough emotional stuff. It was his idea we move back to the village and he moved companies and retrained to relocate his job.

Since becoming a Christian I have found a sense of peace which I could never quite find before. I'm learning to pray about everything, which helps me grow in faith and also helps with any anxiety. I joined a weekly Bible study group in January 2018 made up of members of the church's congregation and we are going from strength to strength. I volunteered with the church's new youth group for eleven- to fourteen-year-olds for four months and in September I was asked to volunteer at the church's weekly toddler group. I read the Bible almost every day either via an App, daily devotional email or the actual leather-bound version which belonged to my dad. I am part of a church community in which Jack is growing and learning and I have been given the opportunity to volunteer and help people. I know one day I will see Grace, Mum and Dad again. I feel as though the pieces of my life's jigsaw are fitting together; my life matters and is part of God's plan.

9

Using BYLYHM in Talks

t had been a busy and very fruitful day as I had spoken at a
church in Cambridge. The church had put on an amazing carol
service and had worked hard at inviting their friends. Of the
1000 people in attendance that day 250 were guests. I was
feeling encouraged as I had delivered my Christmas talk and
really felt I had connected with the people.

I had spoken twice already and was relaxing as I prepared for the third
meeting in the evening which was my final talk of the year. All three talks were
evangelistic and so at the end of each one I delivered my Big Yes, Little Yes,

Healthy Maybe appeal (I will show my "script" later in this chapter). The young adults' pastor came to see me and told me how he was really encouraged and he wanted to thank me. The reason for this is he had invited his friend (who was an atheist) to the carol service. It wasn't the first time he had invited him to something but this was different. He told me that at previous gospel talks he had invited his friend to, he left with no real means of chatting to his friend about the response as they tended to be about first-time commitments or recommitments. He told me that for the first time ever he could talk to his friend because of the Healthy Maybe. I was thrilled to hear this.

I think it is important to use the Big Yes, Little Yes, Healthy Maybe approach to our talks. It is really crucial that we actively encourage and facilitate those who bring their friends along to hear the gospel preached in their personal evangelism. It's easy to get so focused on the first time commitments – the Big Yes – that we don't value the Little Yes or the Healthy Maybe.

God Appealing Through Me

When it comes to making evangelistic appeals in my talks, God has definitely made some tweaks as to how I do this! I have been deeply impacted by 2 Corinthians 5:11–21 throughout my ministry: "We are therefore Christ's ambassadors, as though God were making his appeal through us" (v. 20). Now I know that it refers to much more than evangelistic appeals but the direct application that God made to me certainly was within the context of appeals. You see up till this time I had invited people to respond to what they had heard or what I had said, however it's not me that people should be responding to but rather God. I started to say in my appeals that God was calling them to follow him, that he was appealing to them to put their life in his hands. As I began to get greater clarity about that moment, the Big Yes, Little Yes, Healthy Maybe language began to develop. I detail below the appeal I was leading when God dropped this language into my heart. For clarity's sake, up until this point I'd only ever invited people to make a first-time commitment to God with an occasional "if you'd like to find out more, talk to the people that brought you". I have to say I began to become dissatisfied with this as I felt like it looked like I wasn't valuing those who weren't ready to become a Christian.

In Chapter 1 of this book I encouraged you to reflect over this passage as a means of motivation and that is because it has rich insights that can inform your evangelism. Several parts of it really informed my appeals. As I have said, the verse is more than just about appeals but it certainly applies to us every time we speak evangelistically.

> *Since, then, we know what it is to fear the Lord, we try to persuade others ... So from now on we regard no one from a worldly point of view ... All this is from God, who reconciled us to himself through Christ and gave us this ministry of reconciliation ... that God was reconciling the world to himself in Christ, not counting people's sins against them. And he has committed to us the message of reconciliation ... We are therefore Christ's ambassadors, as though God were making his appeal through us.*

Oh – my – goodness, if that doesn't excite us I don't know what does. We have an incredible privilege to represent God.

I honestly believe that every time we preach the reconciling message of the gospel God is appealing through us. It was this revelation that stopped me inviting people to respond to what they had heard – "What will you do with what you have heard today?" – and I started my appeals with the phrase, "God is calling you to put your life in his hands, he is appealing to you right now to follow him ..." This was because I began to realise God wants me to:

- Try to persuade.
- See no one as unsaveable (view no one from a world perspective).
- Be used by him to reconcile people.
- Use the message of reconciliation he has placed in our hands.
- Be his ambassador.
- Realise he is making his appeal through me.

The Script

Even before Big Yes, Little Yes, Healthy Maybe had developed in me it was clear to me that ever since I have been an evangelistic minister there was a need to challenge people to *look closer* – I carried this passion wherever I spoke, aware that, as my friend J.John often says, "Most people's understanding of Christianity is actually a misunderstanding." In my early days of evangelistic speaking I did lots of schools work and in the assemblies and lessons I spoke much about "Look closer because things aren't always what they seem and if you are going to say, 'Christianity is not for me', at least know what it is you are saying isn't for me."[15] As the conviction that half the battle we face is changing the perceptions many have of the Christian faith began to grow in me so did my dissatisfaction with my appeals. I would go for Big Yes (and still do by the way) but I would feel the need to allow people to investigate and so would invite people to speak to the person who invited them. As I said earlier, I felt it looked a little bit like I was only interested in the Big Yes! Why so? I would invite those who said the Big Yes to come and meet me at the door so I could give them something, but the others, well, they had to just see their friend! Now I know it's not all about me, but I did feel it presented something

Half the battle we face is changing the perceptions many have of the Christian faith.

that wasn't true. You see I really value the Healthy Maybe and the Little Yes and want to celebrate and encourage it because that is, as I have referenced regularly throughout this book, the way most people come to follow Christ. I began to pray more about it and then one day, when I was doing an appeal, I felt a really strong nudge and that moment the Big Yes, Little Yes, Healthy Maybe was born. In this particular event I was going to use my normal type of appeal but that's not what came out of my mouth. The interesting thing is that day and since I have seen more people respond to the gospel than ever, including an increase of first-time commitments. From that moment I have continued to use the words and definitions God gave me ...

> *God is calling you to put your life in his hands and to follow him. All he requires is a heartfelt "yes" from you. Saying yes to God is about saying sorry for living life your way and leaving him out of your life. Saying yes is about thanking God for sending Jesus to die on the cross so you can be forgiven. Saying yes to God is about turning away from living life your way and with his help living life his way. It's like you're saying a Big Yes to God. If that's you, why don't you say "yes" to God right now, not out loud but in the quietness of your own heart and mind?*

> *– PAUSE –*

> *It might be that you are here today and you are saying I'm not ready to say the Big Yes to God, but you know you need to look into Christianity. Why don't you make an intentional decision to find out more? It's like you are saying a Little Yes. You may be saying it to God but you may simply be saying it to yourself. Why don't you say "I'm a Little Yes" in the stillness and quietness of your own heart and mind?*

> *– PAUSE –*

> *It might be that you are here today and you are saying I'm not ready to say the Big Yes or the Little Yes but I wonder if I can ask if you are open minded about God? If you are, would you be willing to make a commitment to remain so and if you aren't, would you be willing to become open minded about God? It's like you're saying "maybe there is something in this". I'm simply asking you to make it a Healthy Maybe. A Healthy Maybe is a willingness to stay open minded about God and Christianity and maybe choose to look into it sometime.*

Depending on the type of event I might vary the delivery of it but not really change the content – I might make it more conversational at a meal; I would still deliver the whole thing but it wouldn't be a formal prayer and the definitions would stay the same.

It's worth saying at this stage that the script is more of an idea as to how I use it rather than this is how you must use it. The only thing I ask is that you do stay true to the definitions of Big Yes, Little Yes, Healthy Maybe, so if people hear it more than once there is no confusion.

It's been amazing seeing what's happened. I get people coming up to me at the end of talks saying to me, "I am definitely now a Healthy Maybe", or "I am one of your Little Yeses", or "I said a Big Yes to God today". I remember one person coming to see me at the end of one of my talks saying, "I am really annoyed with you; I can no longer be an atheist because I have to admit there could be a God and that now I have to look into it." He said, "In the space of forty minutes I have gone from a Big No, to a Healthy Maybe and into a Little Yes." I smiled and so did he. This approach helps local ministers best know how to help people along the journey.

Big Yes, Little Yes, Healthy Maybe and Sundays

What I have talked about so far has been very much in the context of delivering an evangelistic talk that is very much presented in the Big Yes, i.e. you are going for a full-on gospel preach with appeal. These are such talks as would mainly be in the types of events I mentioned in the bubbling-along evangelism in Chapter 6. But what about Sundays?

I would like to encourage you to think about writing your Sunday talks with people in mind as opposed to Christians. Often in our churches we have guests in but our talks alienate. Now I realise I say this as someone who doesn't preach week by week in the same church, and that everything I do I see through the eyes of someone who is an evangelist, but I do think we can involve a lot more in our talks about how this all connects to real life. I love and would recommend Andy Stanley's book *Deep and Wide*.[16] It's all about creating a church that non-Christians are happy to come to. He doesn't suggest (nor do I) that everything we do is purely for the guest but he does talk great sense when it comes to acknowledging that there are people present who aren't familiar with what we do.

A number of my minister friends have started doing appeals at the end of their talks for people who are present that aren't Christians. I am thrilled about this but want to just suggest a few things.

1. **So often we alienate the guest** from our opening words, "Turn in your Bible to ..."

2. **Build good space in your introduction** to take hold of as many hands as possible (not literally – that would be weird). Through lots of questions, quotes, illustrations and life chat, I want to connect my talk to as many people as possible, including the guests. I would then read from the Bible, landing it on what I have just talked about. Jesus was particularly good at this. I want to take the people to the Bible not the Bible to the people. By the way, when reading the Bible read it with life and also read relevant not long – focus on what really matters in the section you read from.

3. **When we quote verses** we say, "John 3:16 says ..." Let's just say something along the lines of "There are a few sentences in the Bible that say something about this. For those of you who know your way around the Bible you will know what I mean when I say it can be found in John chapter 3, verse 16."

4. **Ever said this**, "And you know that David was ..."? Actually they don't. Don't assume knowledge.

5. **Make your talks full of words that connect** and then apply to non-Christians first and then Christians second. It can be done – it will take a while but you will get used to it.

6. **If you are an expository preacher**, I encourage you to look at the themes that connect to people outside of the church.

7. **If we do an appeal** but don't connect with them through the talk apart from a quick gospel narrative at the end, are they really listening?

8. **To help them listen**, talk to them all the way through. Have you ever been in a large room when you are all talking and then you say, "Granddad, what do you think?" Turning to Granddad you realise he's asleep or hasn't been listening and so you shout again and expect him to make a sensible reply! I appreciate some people are better at talking to people who aren't Christians but it's always good to learn how to be better. One of my favourite quotes is, "The biggest room in the world is the room for improvement."

9. **In your preparation** look at how you can layer it into your sermons. Better to plan in advance and no one to be present that isn't a Christian than to not plan at all and have them present. Be a pastor to those who know Jesus and those who don't.

If we can begin to connect people in with what we are saying I believe we can begin to create a "Could this be what you need in your life?" application for those who don't know the Lord but will doubtless be Healthy Maybe or Little Yes people by nature of the fact that they have been coming along to church! We have an incredible opportunity to engage those who are in the Little Yes and Healthy Maybe place, as well as those in the Big Yes place.

Big Yes, Little Yes, Healthy Maybe Talks

It has been said to me on many occasions that people sitting down and listening to someone speaking was just not the done thing anymore. All this against the backdrop of more motivational speakers and comedians than ever filling larger venues than ever! People are used to listening to things that entertain or inform or a combination of both. I'm not suggesting that we entertain, but I am suggesting that we make it engaging.

I sometimes run my Reason to Believe series and Life series on Sunday mornings in churches. Reason to Believe is an apologetics-based course which asks the following questions:

> **1.** Is it reasonable to believe the Bible?
>
> **2.** Is it reasonable to believe in a God you can't see?
>
> **3.** Is it reasonable to believe in a God of love in a world of suffering?
>
> **4.** Is it reasonable to believe I can just do what feels right to me?
>
> **5.** Is it reasonable to believe that Christianity is right?

I have also run my Life series, which is an interactive café-style/magazine-style series that talks about purpose. We look at the following:

> **1. Life before it:** are we born for a purpose?
>
> **2. Life during it:** can we live like people with purpose?
>
> **3. Life after it:** is there purpose in death?
>
> **4. Life unlock it:** letting God put his purpose in you.

Of course, all of these talks can be done anytime but why not try it on a Sunday. I was doing one of my "Curry, Comedy and Christianity" events for a church which basically involves hiring an Indian restaurant, eating some curry and then I do a talk around my curry pilgrimage. I am from Bradford and so have got some good stories to tell. One of the members of the church came to see me at the end to tell me that he had invited his friend but he had declined saying, "You joking aren't you, eating food with a lot of people I don't know?"

I said, trying to support him in what I thought was a discouraging moment, "Well, you can only try your best, don't be hard on yourself."

"I'm not," he replied. "He asked me what time church is on Sunday as he wanted to come to that instead."

It doesn't always go according to our plan, does it? Might there be some who would come to church if we did some more life-impacting talks?

I have a bunch of "Celebrate" talks which are for the Sundays nearest to all the festivals throughout the year, for example Mothers' Day, Fathers' Day, Valentine's day, Harvest, Easter and Christmas to name a few. Why not take these and have a Sunday service that just celebrates with families. For example, near to Valentine's Day build your talk around asking, "Could it be that God is the love that we are all looking for ..." These are just a few simple ideas to get you thinking about Big Yes, Little Yes, Healthy Maybe talks. Why not pull together all your creatives and see what you can come up with. Things that inform and people enjoy are, in themselves, good at creating the Healthy Maybe in people. The relational build is so important even here!

The Yes Again

I've experienced over the years people saying Yes Again to God after one of my evangelistic talks. I want to therefore just address this at the close of this chapter.

I try to listen to the Holy Spirit as to whether in my appeals I give opportunity for people to say this – to come back to God or to recommit themselves to God. Of course if you are a local pastor you may well know some of those people where I wouldn't as I am visiting. Again, in your talk preparation think about how you can layer in this content and application in case you have people present who once walked with Jesus or came to church but don't now.

There are four main types of people that I see make a Yes Again decision:

1. The person we have historically classed as the "backslider". This is the type of person who has slipped gradually and lost all faith in God or, at best, all desire to know him. They can often be people who were brought up in church but when they hit the age of being able to decide for themselves, they have done just that.

2. The next group are those that we now call de-churched. I have seen many of this group recommit their lives in a different way. You see they have fallen out of relationship with the church but not with God. This can be due to dissatisfaction with authority or the institution. Now I can hear some people saying "you must go to church" and I agree that church is important but I am trying to make a distinction so that we know how to treat these types of people. I would say, however, that if there isn't anything in your life that actively keeps your faith alive (for example, church) then I do know in some instances where the faith in God has dissipated.

3. This group of people are very different and tend to be amongst those who are new to the Christian faith, although not exclusively so. I've had many people respond to the gospel who have been on such courses as Alpha or Christianity Explained. When I talk to the minister of the church I'm told that they came to faith at said course. I'm really

okay with this as in the early stages of the conversion or decision people haven't yet established a strong sense of assurance of salvation. The truth is, from time to time we can all go through moments when we may not have full assurance.

4. The final group are people who have complicated their faith! I have so many people who say to me, "You just have the ability to simplify what it's all about." It is true that we can very easily clutter our faith and we all, from time to time, need a reminder of what it's all about. I often see people after I've preached the gospel that have recommitted their lives to God, not because they are backslidden, de-churched or lack assurance of salvation, but rather because they have just had new life breathed back into a faith that had become a bit mundane or burdened.

All of these responses are valid and excite me. As people are saying "yes" to God again I think they thrill God too. When people aren't used to hearing the gospel preached it can do wonders for their faith when they do. I have even seen people recommit their lives to Christ when I have been teaching on sharing your faith with people. And do you know what? That's okay.

Why not have a Big Yes, Little Yes, Healthy Maybe space in your church welcome area. Get some Big Yes, Little Yes, Healthy Maybe packs so that you can give appropriate literature as mentioned in Chapter 6. Get a pop-up banner and really make it look nice – show value for the journey. I would encourage you to build bubbling-along evangelism into your culture then let the language of the appeal reflect the culture of the church evangelism strategy.

#WeCan'tCreateSoulsButWeCanCreateJourney

Journey

Janet's story

My name is Janet and I've been a Christian for thirty-five years, but took fifteen years to make the decision! Fortunate to grow up with Christian parents, I had faith modelled to me, with church attendance as the norm. However, "knowing all about it" didn't change anything until someone pointed out, quite directly, that I needed to accept or reject that knowledge for myself. That challenge changed my life, and I'll be forever grateful that someone loved me enough and was bold enough to make it clear a decision was needed, and also gave me an opportunity to do so.

Luke's story

My name is Luke and I have been a Christian for thirty years. The main part of my journey happened over five years. I had a happy childhood in a Christian home but I knew I was just doing what was expected of me. I went to church because my friends and family did. At university, studying science, I met people of all faiths (and none) and learned from them, asking all about their beliefs. I read widely and investigated for myself. For five years I checked and double-checked but the more I researched, the more evidence I found. My conclusion was clear: the gospel was true. Jesus died for me. Mum and Dad were right all along.

Jay's story

My name is Jay and I have been a Christian for eleven years. My journey to Jesus happened over a period of twenty-two years. I first wanted to follow Jesus when I was eleven at Keswick when I snuck into the adults meeting. Then at seventeen I realised I didn't really have a testimony and started to search the Bible for an answer. In 2007 I did a documentary on the murder of three believers in Malatya, Turkey, which led me down a path of realising my own sin and that only Jesus could cleanse me and save me from the trouble I was in. It was in that moment I saw I was a sinner and gave my life to Jesus.

Vicki's story

My name is Vicki and I have been a Christian for fifteen years. It would be easy to think that my journey to Jesus took just two short years from heroin and crack addiction to new life after I arrived on an Alpha course in 2002. It was awesome and powerful and Spirit-filled and life-changing, yes, but in many ways that is much too simplistic. God used so many people and situations to draw me to him over my lifetime, from the people that ran the drop-in that kept me alive, the soup kitchens, the Jesus Army guys on that bus, and the lady who gave me the Bible that the Holy

Spirit used to open my eyes on that wonderful, glorious day when my Saviour spoke so clearly and deeply into my heart in a hostel room: just me, Jesus and the word of God. Looking back I even remember as a tiny child reading the story of the selfish giant, and the beautiful illustration of the tiny Christ-child with holes in his hands that whispered to my heart that even then he was with me.

Deborah's story

My name is Deborah and I have been a Christian for seventeen years. My journey to Jesus happened over several years. I had been in a loveless and mentally abusive marriage for almost twenty years. By the time I reached forty years of age we were heavily in debt through my husband's poor money management. We had exhausted respect for one another, and I had no self-confidence. I cried out to a God I didn't know, asking for things he was never going to give me. Finally, I cried, "Help me!" The effect was immediate. I found courage I was unaware of. I left my marriage and the rest is history! My second husband is God-chosen and it is obvious in all that we are!

Linda's story

My name is Linda and I have been a Christian for fifty-three years. It took me four years to make the decision. I lived in North Africa until I was twelve years old. On a trip home I was invited to a youth club and heard about Nicodemus asking how you can be born again. I returned to Benghazi and thought about that story for two years. When we finally returned to the UK I was taken to church regularly by a friend and one evening, after a sermon was preached and an invitation to give your life to Jesus was made, I responded and that day I became part of the family of God.

Ellen's story

My name is Ellen and I've been a Christian for twenty-three years. My journey to Jesus happened over a period of five years. During my school days, when I was eleven, I met a Christian girl who invited me to youth club. I saw a difference in her and her friends. I had questions about life and wondered if this was really all there was. One time I went to church and had a sense of God being there that's really difficult to describe. Jesus answered the questions I was asking on the inside and I decided I had to follow him.

Neil's story

My name is Neil and I have been a Christian for twenty-five years. My journey to Jesus happened over a period of thirty years. I was born to a violent alcoholic father who had attempted to kill my mum. With swear words in every sentence, I grew up with much anger in my heart. We escaped and Mum started to take me to church. She was angry, too, and I suffered when she had a breakdown. Although I believed in God it was not until after a failed angry marriage that God got a hold of me. After a church meeting I prayed to receive

God into my life and for the Holy Spirit to change me. A few days later I had an amazing experience of the Holy Spirit and since then I have never sworn again – God has taken my anger and replaced it with his love. God has now called me to be a priest in the Anglican Church and given me a beautiful wife and family.

10

Using BYLYHM in Personal Faith-sharing

'd been to a meeting in London and was returning on the 19:20 London Marylebone to Warwick Parkway. I was in the "quiet carriage" setting up my iPad to maximise the time and work on this book. The train was almost ready for leaving and, I'm going to be honest, it was nice as there was only me and a lady opposite me with a table in between.

A couple of people joined talking about *Les Misérables* which they had seen and were saying how amazing it was. Having seen the play myself I could relate to their excitement but this was the quiet carriage, which the lady opposite me reminded them of once they sat down. It didn't seem to affect them as they continued right up to Bicester North, as did the raised eyebrows from the lady opposite me. As we pulled away from the platform the train didn't seem to gather much speed which we were told over the loud speaker was due to the slippery tracks, which raised my eyebrows at the same time as those of my silent companion opposite for the second time. "Isn't it funny," I said, "in this day and age you wouldn't have thought tracks would cause this problem." The conversation travelled quickly onto talking about the problem being that the rolling stock isn't owned by the same company as the tracks and that the companies have different priorities about spending. We visited the notion of it all being owned by the government again and whether that would really help. As we continued to put the train world to rights, I began to realise that she seemed to know more about business stuff than me and I felt that, as I chatted on, I may have been faking it a bit!

I asked her what she did saying, "You seem to know what you are talking about." This lady was a

> **If I've learned one thing about personal evangelism it's this: we need to actively create journey.**

business marketeer and consulted a lot in business settings in London, particularly in brand marketing. She asked me what I did. "I'm in a similar job to you," I said. "I work with an organisation that has five hundred and fifty centres around the UK and we look at issues of community engagement. I consult nationally and locally, helping our centres to connect with their communities and to help their spiritual development." I then told her that it was a church denomination.

Her interest began to rise as she said, "This is fascinating, tell me more."

I explained what I do. I then said I'd created a framework called "Big Yes, Little Yes, Healthy Maybe". She wanted to know more so I told her what it meant, explaining to her that "Big Yes" was for those who want to make a commitment to God; "Little Yes" was for those who wanted to really look into the Christian faith, and that the "Healthy Maybe" was about inviting people to become open minded about God or to remain open minded to God. Just before I explained the "Healthy Maybe" part, I said, "You're going to love this next bit as you will know, in branding, half the battle is changing people's perceptions of the product!" She nodded, very strongly agreeing with the point. I said we face the same battle in the church as many people have a perception about Christianity and/or God which is why I often challenge people about their perception when I am preaching. As I introduced "Healthy Maybe" to her, she loved it. I then asked her, "Where would you consider yourself?" She said she definitely believed in God though she wasn't sure what that was or meant. She did say she was a "Healthy Maybe".

I asked her if she would ever consider becoming a "Little Yes". She said she would but she didn't know how to. I told to her that I could help her if she wanted. By now the train had left Bicester and was approaching Leamington Spa where she would be getting off. She said, "I would love you to help me become a 'Little Yes', I think this meeting was meant to be." We exchanged emails and have arranged to meet up. If I've learned one thing about personal evangelism it's this: we need to actively create journey.

I'm sure you are familiar with the statistic that approximately 85 per cent of people come to faith through a friend. What you may not know is that it's been estimated that within about one year most people lose quality contact with their friends who aren't Christians. We need to be more intentional about connecting with people. Acquaintances happen, friendships are built.

Much of what we have already explored in Big Yes, Little Yes, Healthy Maybe connects as much in a personal level in our evangelism as it does with what we have already journeyed through. I have deliberately left "Using BYLYHM in Personal Faith-sharing" almost to the end of the book because actually it comes down to people like you and me making disciples. I'd like to explore five key areas.

1. Tell Your Story

We live in a world of story. Much of the current advertising we see on TV tells a story as opposed to telling you about the facts. From our very first breath we are told stories. Most of us love a good film, or book, or a good soap. One of my favourite ways of chilling is when I'm with a bunch of mates and the evening is spent all telling our stories. We are surrounded by stories and here's the brilliant thing: we have a story worth telling.

Our personal testimony is our personal story! I totally believe that our testimony is our greatest tool in sharing our faith but I would like to challenge something that I've heard said many times and indeed used to say myself: tell your testimony because they can't deny it! That is true but what people can say is, "Oh, that's nice for you, I'm glad you found faith but it's not for me." I think it shows a naivety simply saying they can't deny it. Just to reaffirm, I'm not saying we shouldn't tell – quite the opposite. I've already stated it's our greatest tool. In fact I am still so convinced of the power of our story that I made a commitment to get mine into print and give it out to 10,000 people – I've only got 4,000 left.

One of the greatest examples of testimony is the man born blind as told in John 9:1–32. It's a great story.

As he went along, he saw a man blind from birth. His disciples asked him, "Rabbi, who sinned, this man or his parents, that he was born blind?"

"Neither this man nor his parents sinned," said Jesus, "but this happened so that the works of God might be displayed in him. As long as it is day, we must do the works of him who sent me. Night is coming, when no one can work. While I am in the world, I am the light of the world." After saying this, he spat on the ground, made some mud with the saliva, and put it on the man's eyes. "Go," he told him, "wash in the Pool of Siloam" (this word means "Sent"). So the man went and washed, and came home seeing.

His neighbours and those who had formerly seen him begging asked, "Isn't this the same man who used to sit and beg?" Some claimed that he was.

Others said, "No, he only looks like him."

But he himself insisted, "I am the man."

"How then were your eyes opened?" they asked.

He replied, "The man they call Jesus made some mud and put it on my eyes. He told me to go to Siloam and wash. So I went and washed, and then I could see."

"Where is this man?" they asked him.

"I don't know," he said.

They brought to the Pharisees the man who had been blind. Now the day on which Jesus had made the mud and opened the man's eyes was a Sabbath. Therefore the Pharisees also asked him how he had received his sight. "He put mud on my eyes," the man replied, "and I washed, and now I see."

Some of the Pharisees said, "This man is not from God, for he does not keep the Sabbath."

But others asked, "How can a sinner perform such signs?" So they were divided.

Then they turned again to the blind man, "What have you to say about him? It was your eyes he opened."

The man replied, "He is a prophet."

They still did not believe that he had been blind and had received his sight until they sent for the man's parents. "Is this your son?" they asked. "Is this the one you say was born blind? How is it that now he can see?"

"We know he is our son," the parents answered, "and we know he *was born blind. But how he can see now, or who opened his eyes, we don't know. Ask him. He is of age; he will speak for himself." His parents said this because they were afraid of the Jewish leaders, who already had decided that anyone who acknowledged that Jesus was the Messiah would be put out of the synagogue. That was why his parents said, "He is of age; ask him."*

A second time they summoned the man who had been blind. "Give glory to God by telling the truth," they said. "We know this man is a sinner."

He replied, "Whether he is a sinner or not, I don't know. One thing I do know. I was blind but now I see!"

Then they asked him, "What did he do to you? How did he open your eyes?" He answered, "I have told you already and you did not listen. Why do you want to hear it again? Do you want to become his disciples too?"

Then they hurled insults at him and said, "You are this fellow's disciple! We are disciples of Moses! We know that God spoke to Moses, but as for this fellow, we don't even know where he comes from."

The man answered, "Now that is remarkable! You don't know where he comes from, yet he opened my eyes. We know that God does not listen to sinners. He listens to the godly person who does his will. Nobody has ever heard of opening the eyes of a man born blind. If this man were not from God, he could do nothing."

To this they replied, "You were steeped in sin at birth; how dare you lecture us!" And they threw him out.

Notice a few things:

They could see there was a difference

"Isn't this the man who used to sit and beg?" (v. 8)

When my dad became a Christian, he would say that on the Sunday evening he didn't really feel hugely different. But when he went to work on the Monday morning and his colleagues asked him if he was okay because he had been at work for a few hours and they hadn't heard him swear, it was then that he realised, as did they, "wasn't this the man who used to...?" Sometimes people who have shared their testimony with the people who knew them well from before they were Christians can often feel it's a hard place, "We know what you used to be like," they would say to them. I say thank God they have seen the change!

They were interested in what and how it happened as well as who did it

"How then were your eyes opened?" (v. 10)

"The Pharisees also asked him how he had received his sight." (v. 15)

"Then they turned again to the blind man, 'What have you to say about him? It was your eyes he opened.'" (v. 17)

Our story and the change that has taken place in us raises an interest in people. They often want to know how it happened and we should share. What we need to learn to do is tell the story not preach it. Make sure we give opportunity for discussion around our story.

"Whether he is a sinner or not, I don't know. One thing I do know. I was blind but now I see!" (v. 25)

We may not be in a place to answer the questions that people have – this man certainly wasn't – but we can tell the truth that there was a time when we couldn't see but now we can. By the way, it is important to seek to answer people's questions when they ask and we will cover that in this chapter a bit later.

Don't go for a Big Yes!

"He answered, 'I have told you already and you did not listen. Why do you want to hear it again? Do you want to become his disciples too?'" (v. 27)

Do you get the sense the chap was getting a bit frustrated? I do. We don't really know why but what they had seen had really knocked them. As they asked around they got no clarity. There may well have been a sense when they came back to him of wanting some answers. They could have been Little Yes people or Healthy Maybe people but he went straight for the Big Yes appeal. We need to learn what our story is and learn to tell it well. Of course some people, like my friend Barry Woodward, tell their story well and God uses it powerfully to see many come to faith, but he is an evangelist! Most of the time in one-to-one settings it doesn't have that impact for all kinds of reasons, one of which is they are in a place to say the Big Yes with Barry and maybe only a Healthy Maybe with you. Let's remember the woman at the well, "Could this be the Messiah?" Isn't it interesting that men believed because she said "Could this be?" which caused them to look into her claims and see for themselves!

Valid as evidence

I was probably a little bit more excited than I should have been when I received my summons to be on jury service. I'd always wanted to be a lawyer or a judge when I was growing up and this was the nearest I was going to get. My mind has always been fascinated by legal cases and evidence and how things were proved. To this day I still love that whole area. On a number of the cases we had no scientific evidence but we were still expected to make a decision purely based on the witness testimonies, which in one case was the punched and the puncher!

We live in a world of recommendations. If I tell my friend I'm planning on eating at a particular restaurant and he's already eaten there, he will give me his opinion. If I respect his culinary expertise I won't eat there if he tells me not to. In fact, there have been many occasions as I travelled around the UK on my way to speak at events that if I mention where I have eaten, people have said, "Oh no, next time eat at ..." If people respect how we live our lives then when we share our story, recommend our faith to them, it will hold more sway.

Testimonies are a great way of showing applied faith. I will always share my testimony with someone on a one-on-one before I share the gospel. After all, our testimony is the gospel applied. So often we preach our testimony rather than tell our story; this is a sure-fire way of putting people off. When we talk about what God has done for us and how he has done it, there is an emotional and spiritual connection with people.

Not only does sharing our story show applied faith but it spreads to the desired life. Many people are looking for life to make sense and when we talk about the many things God has done for us and how he changed it and gave us purpose, it can really speak to a felt need. I'm not suggesting here we offer faith as a magic wand to meet the needs of people but it is one of the benefits of being a Christian. Let me remind you of this verse.

> *Praise the LORD, my soul; all my inmost being, praise his holy name. Praise the LORD, my soul, and forget not all his benefits – who forgives all your sins and heals all your diseases, who redeems your life from the pit and crowns you with love and compassion, who satisfies your desires with good things so that your youth is renewed like the eagle's.* (Psalm 103:1–5)

I've often said that if the only thing that God did for us was to forgive us that would be enough. In one sense that would be and yet the truth is he does so much more than that and we are not presenting the whole of what God is about if we don't talk about "his benefits". Let me encourage you to read "Distortion of the Christian Message" in Chapter 1 again so we don't distort it.

2. Answering Their Questions

So here is a question: "Did Adam have a belly button?" Break up into small groups and discuss!

A good attitude and a good answer

The number-one way we get into conversations as Christians still tends to be when someone asks us a question. And if the conversations don't start that way there probably will be one soon. It's probably the thing we fear the most! We can end up feeling like we are backed into a corner.

Why do we feel that way? Because of that pressure of giving the killer answer that will back the person asking it into *their* corner or, to mix my metaphors for a moment, we want the passing shot in the apologetics game of tennis that will leave our opponent with no means of return. Can I use another metaphor? We end up feeling like it's a verbal sparring match and whoever can land the best punch is going to win. I think we need to have a different view on the way we answer people's questions. It's not about answering so that someone will become a Christian; it's about defending what we believe.

I still agree with the phrase, "Don't win the argument but lose the soul." Let me remind you here of a verse we use a lot when trying to encourage people to be willing to share their faith:

> *But in your hearts revere Christ as Lord. Always be prepared to give an answer to everyone who asks you to give a reason for the hope that you have. But do this with gentleness and respect.* (1 Peter 3:15)

The Greek word here for "answer" is *apologia* from which we get "Apologetics" which is defined as "a systematic defence, or justification, of the divine origin and authority of the Christian faith".[17]

I find the word "systematic" here interesting. It denotes methodical; in other words it's not something we blurt out when we are asked a question we didn't expect. Again our reference from 1 Peter encourages the "always", "prepared" and "everyone" principle. A challenge but one we can rise to nevertheless.

Notice it's a defence not an attack, highlighted by the end of 1 Peter 3:15, "gentleness and respect", and further emphasised again in Colossians 4:5,6: "Be wise in the way you act towards outsiders; make the most of every opportunity. Let your conversations be always full of grace, seasoned with salt, so that you may know how to answer everyone." These verses aren't discouraging good answers but they are encouraging a good attitude as well.

So have you worked it out yet? Did Adam have a belly button?

You may be thinking at this point that I have lost my theological mind! So let me put you out of your misery.

Many years ago I learned a valuable lesson when I was doing some open-air work in the centre of Bristol just opposite Wesley's (chapel for those of you who know it). I had got into conversation with a man and he asked me a question – you got it, "Did Adam have a belly button?"

I said to the man, "I am not going to lie to you, I have never been asked that question before." (Now, to be honest, I've never been asked it since!) I said to the man if he could give me a couple of minutes I would have a think and give him an answer, which I said may or may not be correct. He agreed.

When I had collected my thoughts I approached him saying, "Right, here is my answer: I don't think Adam had a belly button because he wasn't born by natural means." The man thanked me for not laughing at him, explaining to me that he had tried to read the Bible many times but he had a few problems which he couldn't get beyond and whenever he asked people who he knew were Christians they had always laughed at him and said, "Why do you keep asking stupid questions?" He told me that he thought my answer was great and then he went on to ask me some of the others he had. We must have spent two hours chatting and we got on to talking about Jesus and I explained the gospel to him. He didn't become a Christian but he definitely became what I now call a Healthy Maybe. I learned a very valuable lesson that day: I will never treat anyone's questions as stupid.

> *One of the teachers of the law came and heard them debating. Noticing that Jesus had given them a good answer, he asked him, "Of all the commandments, which is the most important?"* (Mark 12:28)

Similar to my experience with the previous man, Jesus was being asked questions by the Pharisees, Herodians and Sadducees who really were just trying to trip him up if you read a few verses earlier – a classic case of the "red herring". Because of the great answers Jesus gave, even though he knew they were trying to trap him, one of the teachers of the law had seen how Jesus handled them and what they were asking, and so he asked, "Of all the commandments, which is the most important?" Now what is significant about this question is that it was one of the most asked questions of the day. So here's the thing, because Jesus had answered well those who tried to trap him with questions, this teacher of the law wanted to know what Jesus thought about the bigger issues of the day.

I firmly believe and have experienced that when we learn to give good answers, when it comes to the bigger issues of the day our friends will come to us. I say this not in unfounded hope but rather through personal experience among my friends who don't know the Lord.

A good approach

When I was at school my maths teacher told us that when we are doing maths we should show our working out because even if we got the answer wrong we could still get marks for our working out. The idea behind this was that we can understand the process but maybe through error get the conclusion wrong. For many of us we can end up disagreeing with people's conclusions but in truth we haven't gone through the process. We can end up knowing what we believe but not necessarily why we believe. I've heard many people say "because the Bible says ..." as they try to answer people's questions. Don't get me wrong, I'm not saying we shouldn't quote the Bible but what I am saying is we have to start from a different place. Let me give you an example:

Enquirer: How can you believe in a God of love in a world of suffering?

Christian: Ah well, you see, when God created the world he created it perfect but then Adam and Eve sinned and so death and suffering and sin entered the world.

Now three key things are a problem here:

- We've based our answer on an assumed knowledge. We think they know the Bible and the story of creation.

- We've based our answer on an assumed objection. We've presumed this is an intellectual question and not an emotional one – that they are asking it because they have an intellectual interest in the answer as opposed to the fact that they are going through some suffering and don't understand why God would allow this!

- We have based our answer on an assumed authority. We think that they accept the Bible as their primary authority.

Whenever someone asks me a question, the first thing I do is to ask them why they are asking the question. Once they have done that I can know for definite what they are really asking and why they are asking it. Once I am satisfied they are coming from a place of intellectual objection then I will start to answer.

I then push the question to its logical conclusion. Now this is a bit of a learned art but I will give you an example.

I was delivering a sixth-form lesson in a school. My brief was to do twenty minutes presentation and then throw it open for questions. I could see the young man on the front row was not in agreement with anything I said and so it came as no surprise that his hand was up first at question time. "Yes please," I said to him.

"The problem with you Christians," he said – I braced myself – "is that you only believe what you read in a book and what people tell you."

I looked at him and said, "Correct." (Now I know it's about the inner witness of the Holy Spirit but I just didn't think he'd understand that and, again, that would be making some assumptions I've advised against earlier). He was shocked as he expected me to deny it or argue against it but here I was agreeing with him. He didn't know what to do and so he started to ask, "Is it really?"

I said, "Well, you said it not me." I asked him if I could ask him a question, which he agreed to. "What do you believe?" I asked. He explained to me what he believed in, to which I asked, "Where did you get that from?"

He said, "Well it's true, isn't it?" I suggested to him that wasn't what I was asking. This happened several times and so I said, "Look, answer my question properly – where did you get that from?" He didn't have time to inhale let alone exhale when a voice from the back of the class shouted out, "He got it from a book!"

I looked at him and asked, "You didn't?" (although, of course, I knew he did). He looked at me somewhat sheepishly saying, "I did." I asked him how it was okay for him to believe what he believed when he got it from a book or it was something someone told him, but it wasn't alright from me to believe what I believe because I got it from a book. He said, "Well the Bible's a load of rubbish, isn't it?" I assured him it wasn't and we would deal with that after the lesson as there were other people wanting to ask questions but would he concede that his first objection wasn't fair? To be fair to him, he did in front of the class. When we chatted after he said he was more open minded now because "you have thought this through more than me". By showing him the process to my conclusion he was willing to be a Healthy Maybe.

I am not saying that by answering people's questions it will make them say the Big Yes but what I am saying is that giving good answers is definitely a key part of enabling people to be a Healthy Maybe as they see us thinking about it more than they do. Many people know what they believe but not always why they believe, and that includes Christians. We can show what we believe and why we believe it, i.e. that we have gone through a process to our conclusions.

I have known people give their lives to Christ when I had answered their question. This wasn't because they had conceded academic defeat but rather because the obstacle to them coming to Christ had been removed – the question was hindering them saying the Big Yes. Undeniably Big Yes, Little Yes, Healthy Maybe is definitely advanced through giving people good answers.

Knowledge Circle – is it possible?

A tool I came across many years ago was what I have called the "Knowledge Circle". I wrote a leaflet on it (it was one of the leaflets that God used to help Dave the designer you will read about later in this chapter). It is really useful for developing the Healthy Maybe and I have used it to good effect over the past twenty-five years. Originally it was created to help atheists in that just because God is outside of your knowledge it doesn't mean he doesn't exist. First I draw a circle.

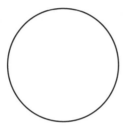

As I draw this circle I say, "Imagine that this circle contains the knowledge of the whole world. All the things that you and I know alongside everything else that is known." I then say to the person, "Here is my pen. Now place a mark in the circle that represents all that you know in comparison to what everyone else knows." Most people would place a dot like the one in the illustration below.

I then confirm that the dot represents everything you have knowledge of but, as you can see, there is a lot you don't know. Is it possible that God exists but that you just don't have knowledge of him? I have known atheists move to agnostics after showing them this.

From this you could tell your testimony. You could use it to share the gospel as per the five points I mention in the next section. Sometimes I have used it along these lines:

> • Is it possible that God exists but you don't know it?
>
> • Is it possible that Jesus died and rose again but you don't know it?
>
> • Is it possible that Christianity is all true but you don't know it?

I would individually talk more about these with some apologetics-style evidence. Sometimes I use it with Big No people as well. I talk a bit more about those at the end of this chapter. I think if we can move people along and they become Healthy Maybe then that's great.

I list some resources at the end of this book to help you get better at handling the objections and the objector to the gospel.

3. Sharing the Message

My friend Tim (not his real name) came to see me once. He was going out with someone who was a recovering alcoholic and was in the twelve-step programme, during which the attendees are encouraged to call on a higher power. My friend who was supporting his partner wanted to talk to me about this higher power and he thought I might be able to help. Now many of us would have been tempted at this point to give Tim absolutely everything, however my time was tight so I said to my friend, "Look, I think you feel this higher power in some way, don't you?"

"I'm not sure but I think so, yes," he said.

"Well, look, why don't we meet up in the next few weeks and I think I can help you discover who that is, would that be good?" I suggested. He said it would so we arranged to meet up and I told him that I believe this higher power is God and that he wants to connect with us. As time was slipping away I said, "I'd love to help you know what it takes to connect with God so let's meet up again and talk." He was happy to do that and so we did, and over several meetings I was able to explain the whole gospel in a way that wasn't rushed but also in a way that he wanted. Let us work to actively create journey in our conversations as opposed to trying to shoehorn and cram the gospel in without really communicating it.

What we say

In terms of what I share and when, I would tend to start with where my friend is; for example, if my friend was aware of their wrong I would tend to start at Jesus' forgiveness on the cross. I find that when I break the gospel into chunks it makes it easier to connect with where someone is at and aids better understanding and memory of it. Remember when I quoted Laurence in Chapter 4 about the one-ton messages? This is where we can begin to develop that. I have essentially five points of the gospel which I share:

i. God's plan: I think it's important to talk about how God's plan is for us to have a relationship with him. I stay away from debating creation and evolution as it tends to get us nowhere. I often say to people I am not going to focus on *how* I got here; I have enough trouble knowing what I do now I *am* here. I talk about how God has a purpose for us.

ii. Our problem: I talk about how our problem is that we have chosen to live life our way and not God's way and that has disconnected us from God and his plan and purpose for our lives; as a result we do a whole bunch of things that God is not happy with and, in truth, we aren't happy with either. I tend not to use the word "sin" as it has so many unhelpful connotations but if you must use it, I would encourage you to explain the concept and then use the word. If you mention sin first they are already putting onto it what they think and so miss grasping your explanation.

iii. Our effort: when talking about our effort I think we need to recognise a cultural shift. When we use the God–Man–Sin diagram and show how our sin gets in the way of our efforts to get to God I would suggest some tweaks in order to communicate clearly. First let's remove the word "man" and replace it with "people"! Then we need to realise that we live in a world where more than ever people do more good works but they aren't all doing it because they think it gets them to God. Some are doing it more because that's how we should behave as humans i.e. social responsibility. So if we say, "Your good works won't get you to God" we have a disconnect because inwardly and possibly outwardly they may say, "I am not doing it for that reason." What I tend to say is along these lines, "We put a lot of effort into trying to make sense of life and how we live in the world around us but that can only ever be found in God and a relationship with him and there is nothing we can do that will earn that."

iv. God's solution: this is Jesus not his cross. Jesus said *he* was the way not his cross. Imagine you met me only on my death bed, how could you make a judgement about what I was like in my life? How can we expect people to accept Jesus if they don't know anything about him. For me it's important to talk about the birth, life, death and resurrection of Jesus. I don't hold back from talking about his death but I think it's critical that people accept Jesus the person and not just what he did on the cross.

v. Our response: you will get no Brownie points for guessing what this is about – that's right, Big Yes, Little Yes, Healthy Maybe. Now, let me just say this, when I preach and invite people to respond I do what I have shown you in Chapter 9, but when it comes to the five one-ton messages I will ask people where they are on each individual point e.g. are they Big Yes, Little Yes or Healthy Maybe to Jesus. This can be very revealing.

N.B. If you find yourself helping someone after they have responded to Christ at an event I would take them through the whole gospel using the approach I outlined in "Our response". This way you can be surer of where they are at in the process which will help you with their discipleship journey as referenced in Chapter 2.

How we say it

If what we say is all about the content then how we say it is all about the delivery. It's important to deliver the gospel well in those moments we get to share. I have a simple approach to this:

Point for the head

A simple but clean point for the head that's easy to remember e.g. I might even write this down as I am sharing or even draw it for them.

Story for the heart

First I would look for a story from my life that would help illustrate the point and if I couldn't find one I would look for one or create a story to illustrate. Let me give you an example (tell this in a chill-out way and have a bit if fun about it): "Just imagine you came to my house and we had scrambled eggs for lunch. In the preparation for that, five eggs were good but one was off but, nevertheless, I will put it in. Well that one bad egg is enough to ruin the whole mixture and even kill someone." We're trying to show that a little bit can have a big impact. "Whoever keeps the whole law and yet stumbles at just one point is guilty of breaking all of it" (James 2:10).

Scripture for the soul

I would then use an appropriate scripture as just illustrated with James 2:10. I really believe in the power of the Bible. As I mentioned in Chapter 9 when quoting the Bible in talks, the same applies here – I would say "There is a sentence in the Bible that says ..." as opposed to using book, chapter and verse. I remember lots of Bible verses and references, then I am able to show people where in the Bible they are if I need to. This is particularly good when sharing with people from other faiths and cultures who know their holy book well. It's also a really good discipline. Sadly, with the internet today we know where to find verses so why remember them? It's a great spiritual discipline to learn the scriptures.

The verses I tend to go with are:

God's plan: "'For I know the plans I have for you,' declares the LORD, 'plans to prosper you and not to harm you, plans to give you hope and a future.'" (Jeremiah 29:11)

Our problem: "We all, like sheep, have gone astray, each of us has turned to our own way." (Isaiah 53:6)

Our effort: "For it is by grace you have been saved, through faith – and this is not from yourselves, it is the gift of God – not by works, so that no one can boast." (Ephesians 2:8,9)

God's solution: "For God so loved the world that he gave his one and only Son, that whoever believes in him shall not perish but have eternal life." (John 3:16)

Our response: "Yet to all who did receive him, to those who believed in his name, he gave the right to become children of God." (John 1:12)

Of course you may have your own. I use these ones for particular reasons but there is no shortage of verses in the Bible to explain the gospel. Have a look at Romans chapters 1 to 11. It used to be known as the Roman Road and there are verses in there you will recognise. When you use the Bible just be aware of any "religious" words you may need to explain, e.g. grace, saved, and so on.

The final step in the delivery is that I wrap my own testimony around each of the five points e.g. Our problem: "I realised that I had lived life my own way and not God's way." By doing this I am applying it to me and if it feels right in the conversation (and most of the time I do this) I would apply it to them by saying something like, "If you acknowledge that you have lived life your way and not God's way then this is part of the journey in connecting with God.

4. Offer to Pray

I want to briefly talk about praying for people at this stage. As the relational build strengthens, you may find people share some of their personal challenges with you. If you feel it is right then why not offer to pray? I certainly have done this and there have been some lovely moments where I've felt something.

Just because someone lets you pray for them it doesn't necessarily mean they are going to become a Christian. I've known people being healed through prayer and they didn't give their lives to God. If you have tried everything and it hasn't worked, then you are willing for anything if it could work. That said, I have known people who have been healed and have received Christ as a result. I have also known people not get healed but feel something and so have then given their lives to Christ. So how does Big Yes, Little Yes, Healthy Maybe connect with the miraculous?

> *Later Jesus appeared to the Eleven as they were eating; he rebuked them for their lack of faith and their stubborn refusal to believe those who had seen him after he had risen. He said to them, "Go into all the world and preach the gospel to all creation. Whoever believes and is baptised will be saved, but whoever does not believe will be condemned. And these signs will accompany those who believe: in my name they will drive out demons; they will speak in new tongues; they will pick up snakes with their hands; and when they drink deadly poison, it will not hurt them at all; they will place their hands on people who are ill, and they will get well."*
>
> *After the Lord Jesus had spoken to them, he was taken up into heaven and he sat at the right hand of God. Then the disciples went out and preached everywhere, and the Lord worked with them and confirmed his word by the signs that accompanied it.* (Mark 16:20)

So Jesus promised what would happen, he commanded them to go, they went and did what he said and Jesus' promise was fulfilled. I believe a key reason why I don't see as many people healed is that I simply don't pray for people. This is something I am journeying towards personally and in my evangelistic ministry, as I build it around relevant words, caring actions and spirit empowered, and fusing it with Big Yes, Little Yes, Healthy Maybe.

What do signs do? They point someone towards something or somewhere. I think we have always expected the miraculous to be the defining moment, and it may well be, but my reading is that it follows the preaching of the gospel and then points to God and maybe leaves people wondering what it is all about. The truth is, as I often say, if Jesus can walk in front of people and they still aren't convinced he is God, then we should understand that people may not receive Christ at the moment they experience something supernatural but it may cause them to investigate (Little Yes) or at least be willing to consider (Healthy Maybe) the God they have just experienced in some way.

5. Links in a Chain

I was taking some text around, along with some of my own leaflet design samples, so that Alan's designer could redesign them and then they would print them professionally for me. I was really pleased, as was my wife, for our back room resembled a printers more than a dining room. The distant noise of the laser printer was constant as I tried to keep on top of what I needed. Alan had become a Christian a few months earlier during one of my evangelistic talks and, full of gratitude to God, he wanted to help me get the message out. I went round on the Monday and Alan introduced me to Dave who was his designer. We had some initial banter about Dave becoming a Christian but essentially Dave was adamant he wouldn't. It was all healthy banter as I said to Dave, "Just watch, you will read those leaflets as you design them and it will all fit together." A bit more banter ensued and then I headed off. A couple of weeks later I headed back to collect the printed item – I was very excited. Dave gave me a hand with the boxes as there were forty thousand leaflets. Okay now my back room was going to resemble a self-storage unit, so still not a dining room. "Never mind, at least the printer noise has gone," I said to Emma.

As Dave and I carried the boxes to my car he told me that through reading the leaflets everything about Christianity fell into place and so he gave his life to Christ (there was a prayer in one of the leaflets). He told me that when he was at university he had a friend who basically said that he wanted to tell Dave all that he believed as a Christian but that once he had told him he wouldn't say anything again unless Dave asked; he stayed true to his word. And now many years later, what his friend had shared and lived had combined with the leaflets and now he had become a Christian – how good is that? That's links in a chain!

I find this passage interesting in so many ways. Moses is in a conversation with God (in a burning bush) as to why he shouldn't go where God is sending him. He gives all kinds of reasons and each time God answers him. I pick it up at Exodus 4:1–9.

> Moses answered, "What if they do not believe me or listen to me and say, 'The LORD did not appear to you'?"
>
> Then the LORD said to him, "What is that in your hand?"
>
> "A staff," he replied.
>
> The LORD said, "Throw it on the ground."
>
> Moses threw it on the ground and it became a snake, and he ran from it. Then the LORD said to him, "Reach out your hand and take it by the tail." So Moses reached out and took hold of the snake and it turned back into a staff in his hand. "This," said the LORD, "is so that they may believe that the LORD, the God of their fathers – the God of Abraham, the God of Isaac and the God of Jacob – has appeared to you." Then the LORD said, "Put your hand inside your cloak." So Moses put his hand into his cloak, and when he took it out, the skin was leprous – it had become as white as snow. "Now put it back into your cloak," he said. So Moses put his hand back into his cloak, and when he took it out, it was restored, like the rest of his flesh.
>
> Then the LORD said, "If they do not believe you or pay attention to the first sign, they may believe the second. But if they do not believe these two signs or listen to you, take some water from the Nile and pour it on the dry ground. The water you take from the river will become blood on the ground."

Moses was concerned about whether they would believe him, listen to him and challenge him. Understandable fears we all face. God then did a bit of chatting to Moses and threw in some supernatural stuff, and then God says a really interesting thing in verses 8 and 9. He basically said to Moses, "If they don't listen the first time, they may listen the second, but then if they don't listen or pay attention to those ..."

I mean, God knew, right? Why didn't he just list what would happen and then say to Moses once that all happened you are good to go? So here's what I think: God has timing and so do humans, which God knows, but Moses doesn't need to and neither do we!

As for the burning bush, the leprous hand and the staff into a serpent and then back again? I think God was showing to Moses what I believe about evangelism and mission and that is: it's not a human enterprise; it's a divine operation.

6. The Big No

I've found myself speaking in all kinds of situations in my ministry down through the years. One such event, about twenty-five years ago, was a barn dance (after it not during it!). It was the end of the event and I was in my customary position by the door ready to meet people who might want to chat some more. A man walked towards me and I could tell he wasn't happy. "The problem with you Christians," he said, "is you believe blindly." He went on with his aggression to say, "I want proof and then I will believe." I asked him what kind of proof he wanted. We chatted and he calmed down a bit and, as he did, he said to me, "Unless God stands in front of me I will not believe." I asked him how he would know it was God that was standing in front of him. He replied, "Well I guess he would introduce himself."

"So let me get this right," I said, "all it would take is for God to stand in front of you and say 'Hi, I'm God' and you would believe." He assured me this was all that was required. I went on to say I still didn't think that he would believe. He started being a bit more cross again. "Why do you say that?" he asked. I went on to explain that 2,000 years ago God turned up on our planet and introduced himself: some believed and some didn't.

I do believe that there are people who will say no even when facing God himself. You may find it frustrating that people in your family don't believe; I find it the same. John 7:5 tells us that even Jesus' own brothers did not believe in him. Now that's hard to get your head around but it reminds us that the greatest proof anyone could ever have – God standing in front of them – would not necessarily mean people will believe. Whilst I have dealt with this in my brain, it's not so straight forward in my heart – it still makes me sad.

> **I do believe that there are people who will say no even when facing God himself.**

Let me also add at this stage that even when someone says a Big No, it isn't necessarily a position they will hold forever. There are times when we meet people in evangelism who are definitely not in any way seeming to be Big Yes, Little Yes or Healthy Maybe people but I hold out in hope and I do so for a reason.

I remember chatting to someone at the end of one of my Reason to Believe courses. He told me that his father, who had been an out-and-out atheist all his life and believed that science gave him all the answers he needed, was now in the place where his belief about science fell short. His wife had passed away and it couldn't help him in the despair he was now feeling as he was asking inwardly what life was all about. He had requested a Bible!

I was speaking at an evangelistic service and before I got up to speak a man shared his testimony. As I listened to him tell his story I laughed out loud when he said, "I was as surprised as anyone when I became a Christian. Even now, after a few years, I still can't believe I'm a Christian." He went on to tell us that before he became a Christian he was an atheist and wasn't the slightest bit interested in God or religion and he wasn't even sure how it all happened.

A number of years ago I met a man who had always come to church with his wife out of love for her as opposed to love for God. He described himself as agnostic until his wife passed away and then for the first time ever he started to look into it for himself. "I'm not quite there yet," he said, "but I think it's only a matter of time." I asked him why he started to look into it for himself. He told me, "Science has given me all the answers I needed." All of a sudden he found himself in a place where his science didn't have an answer for him. I met him again a few years later and he was following Jesus and making up for lost time.

It is my firm opinion that God is always on our case as he wants us to know him. We're reminded in 2 Peter 3:9, "The Lord is not slow in keeping his promise, as some understand slowness. Instead he is patient with you, not wanting anyone to perish, but everyone to come to repentance." Similarly 2 Samuel 14:14 tells us, "Like water spilled on the ground, which cannot be recovered, so we must die. But that is not what God desires; rather, he devises ways so that a banished person does not remain banished from him."

Right up till the last breath God is working to bring people to him. Only heaven will know how many Big No people become Big Yes at that moment. I've certainly heard enough stories to fill this book with people who accepted Christ in the final days and moments.

Luke 23:32–43 is the account of the final moments of two people crucified with Jesus.

> *Two other men, both criminals, were also led out with him to be executed. When they came to the place called the Skull, they crucified him there, along with the criminals – one on his right, the other on his left. Jesus said, "Father, forgive them, for they do not know what they are doing." And they divided up his clothes by casting lots. The people stood watching, and the rulers even sneered at him. They said, "He saved others; let him save himself if*

he is God's Messiah, the Chosen One." The soldiers also came up and mocked him. They offered him wine vinegar and said, "If you are the king of the Jews, save yourself."

There was a written notice above him, which read: THIS IS THE KING OF THE JEWS.

One of the criminals who hung there hurled insults at him: "Aren't you the Messiah? Save yourself and us!" But the other criminal rebuked him. "Don't you fear God," he said, "since you are under the same sentence? We are punished justly, for we are getting what our deeds deserve. But this man has done nothing wrong." Then he said, "Jesus, remember me when you come into your kingdom." Jesus answered him, "Truly I tell you, today you will be with me in paradise."

I love the fact that the one who received Christ preached the gospel to the other before he asked Jesus to remember him when he comes into his kingdom. I wonder if as he spoke the truth about Jesus' death and his own state that he suddenly realised. This is just my thoughts, but what I do know is that in the dying thief's final moments he surrendered his life in a personal moment with Jesus.

I've known many people receive Christ as they take their final breaths on this planet. What may seem a Big No in the moments of our faith-sharing may not be the final decision a person makes about Christ: we have a wonderful opportunity to give people everything they need to know to give their life to God.

#WeCan'tCreateSoulsButWeCanCreateJourney

FINAL THOUGHTS
Matthew's Mathematics

I took the decision to leave the north of England where I was born and brought up. I wasn't expecting to leave Huddersfield where we had moved to from Bradford any time soon but out of the blue God opened the opportunity to move to Warwickshire which has been such a good move. Up until this move I'd been surrounded by loads of great friends and so whenever I needed help with anything I was spoilt for choice.

We moved to the beautiful town of Kenilworth just a few days before Christmas (yes, it was the best time to move!). We got a few things unpacked to give us enough to get going. My wife Emma made an amazing job of cosying up an area around the fire in the sitting room and we made it feel as much like Christmas as we could.

We had just one child at that time and she was only eight months old so it had its challenges trying to settle in as we began the long process of unpacking boxes. The meticulous labelling was compromised on the basis that the removal company hadn't been accurate with the size of lorry required, the result being that from the word go we were against it as they sourced another removal company to meet the deficit in box space! All this meant that we arrived several hours later than we planned, with my Rover 75 having just about enough space for me to drive it. With just five minutes to spare before the estate agents closed, I dumped my car on double-yellow lines and sprinted to pick up the key. Then it was across to our new home with boxes already being unpacked and, despite our best efforts, they ended up being where they shouldn't. Well, as you can imagine, it wasn't plan A.

If you have ever moved you will know it's stressful enough, even when everything goes well. Our problem was that not only had it not gone well but we had a little girl to take care of. One of us had to look after her whilst the other spent time navigating the boxes. I remember thinking to myself several days in, as the boxes that were labelled "upstairs main bedroom" were not in the bedroom but rather in the outside shed (I'm still not entirely sure how they got there), we need some help. I started to actually do the sums in my head. If I could find someone to help we could find the lost items twice as quickly and probably find more lost items along the way as we doubled the search effort. I quickly scaled it up: imagine if I had four, six, eight or even more, that would be fantastic. The more people we could get looking, the more lost things we would find and the quicker we would find them. I could only dream as I plodded along making little headway.

> *Jesus went through all the towns and villages, teaching in their synagogues, proclaiming the good news of the kingdom and healing every disease and illness. When he saw the crowds, he had compassion on them, because they were harassed and helpless, like sheep without a shepherd. Then he said to his disciples, "The harvest is plentiful but the workers are few. Ask the Lord of the harvest, therefore, to send out workers into his harvest field."* (Matthew 9:35–38)

I work on the basis that God is at work in lots of people and places. I've lost count of the number of people who have contacted me on Facebook or by letter or I have met who became Christians years previously when I spoke at an event they came to as a non-Christian. I didn't even know about them receiving Christ. Add to this those that I do know about and I can safely say, "The harvest is plentiful."

I wanted to end the book at the same place I began, that being that God is the Lord of the harvest and the more people we get looking the quicker we will find the lost, those who are like sheep without a shepherd. Just as Jesus went about his every day he found them because he went intentionally looking. Remember this verse: "For the Son of Man came to seek and to save the lost" (Luke 19:10).

He is the Lord of the harvest and it is totally down to him in terms of revealing himself to people. I am also reminded he uses us to harvest what he has grown. The King James Version of the Bible calls us "labourers". If you have ever watched labourers on a building sight, they don't always get to see it all finished and it's really hard work. *As* we say Up North, "We have to put a shift in." But let's see ourselves as privileged people and not just hired hands.

Sir Christopher Wren was an English anatomist, astronomer, geometer and mathematician-physicist, as well as one of the most highly acclaimed English architects in history. He was given the responsibility for rebuilding fifty-two churches in the City of London after the Great Fire in 1666. There are many stories told about his greatest achievement, St Paul's Cathedral.

One story I love is how he was interested in the attitudes of the labourers as the cathedral was being built. He went around asking them what they were doing. The replies were varied and yet the same: "I'm moving stone", "I'm cutting wood", "I'm mixing cement". He asked one person, however, and their reply was fantastic: "I am building a magnificent cathedral."

It's very easy to get bogged down in the mundanities of life and even our faith – "I'm going to church", "I'm paying the mortgage" – and yet we are building a magnificent cathedral. I remind you again that one of my life phrases and prayers is, "Lord, help me to move from pressure to privilege." We all know we ought to pray more, share more, give more, but I want to live my life for God out of a sense of privilege not pressure.

It's been estimated that it takes the average person five years to come to Christ. Well I don't know how accurate it is but what I do know is it's a journey and that for many people they go through the Big Yes, Little Yes, Healthy Maybe stages and we get the joy of being a link in that chain as the Holy Spirit works in them and through us. When I fully grasp this I become more aware of the privilege that God wants to use me. Sharing my faith becomes more of a "Wow, I get to do this" and less of a "Sigh, I have to do this".

As I end this book I offer this prayer for the church:

Dear Lord of the harvest, please send out workers into the harvest field, helping me to lead by example, fully assured that you are indeed at work, and ever thankful that I get to join you on your mission. Amen.

#WeCan'tCreateSoulsButWeCanCreateJourney

Notes

Notes

Endnotes

1. Tom Wright, *Paul: A Biography* (SPCK, 2018). For those of you who don't know, Tom Wright is also known as N.T. Wright (depending upon whether he is writing academic or popular theology) and is acknowledged as "the world's leading New Testament scholar" (*Newsweek*).

2. Shane Claiborne, *The Irresistible Revolution: Living as an Ordinary Radical* (Zondervan, 2006).

3. Bill Hull, *Conversion and Discipleship: You Can't Have One Without the Other* (Zondervan, 2016).

4. Steven Emery-Wright and Ed Mackenzie, *Networks for Faith Formation: Relational Bonds and the Spiritual Growth of Youth* (Eugene, OR: Wipf & Stock, 2017).

5. For further reading: Ed Mackenzie, 'Generative Catechesis: Teaching the faith to the next generation' in Cory Seibel (ed.), *Generative Church: A Global Conversation about Investing in Emerging Generations* (Eugene, OR: Wipf and Stock, 2019).

6. Alan Hirsch, *The Forgotten Ways: Reactivating the Missional Church* (Brazos Press, a division of Baker Publishing Group, 2006).

7. Prochaska, J. and DiClemente, C., "Stages and Processes of Self-change in Smoking: toward an integrative model of change", (1983). In *Journal of Consulting and Clinical Psychology*, 5, pages 390–395.

8. Wikipedia accessed February 2019 https://en.wikipedia.org/wiki/C._S._Lewis

9. First published in 1975 – Professor Dr James F. Engel (1934–2016).

10. Laurence Singlehurst, *Sowing, Reaping, Keeping: People-sensitive Evangelism* second edition (IVP, 2006).

11. Singlehurst, *Sowing, Reaping, Keeping*, pages 28–30.

12. *Look Closer: Mark's Gospel* can be found on my website shop at www. revmarkgreenwood.com.

13. http://www.jamiearpinricci.com/2009/06/preach-the-gospel-at-all-times/

14. Ross Hastings, *Missional God, Missional Church* (IVP, 2012).

15. *Look Closer* became the theme of a number of resources I would later develop which you can see on my website.

16. Andy Stanley, *Deep and Wide* (Zondervan, 2016)

17. Walter A. Elwell (ed.), *The Concise Evangelical Dictionary of Theology* (Baker Publishing Group, 1991).

RESOURCES
Further Reading

Here is a reading list to help you explore further some of the issues covered in the book.

Conversion and Discipleship: You Can't Have One Without the Other by Bill Hull (Zondervan, 2016).

Deep and Wide by Andy Stanley (Zondervan, 2016).

Sowing, Reaping, Keeping: People-sensitive Evangelism by Laurence Singlehurst (IVP, 2006).

The Simple Gospel: Understanding and Sharing the Jesus Story by Ben Jack (The Message Trust, 2019).

The Explicit Gospel by Matt Chandler (Crossways, 2014).

The Word's Out: Principles and Strategies for Effective Evangelism Today by Dave Male and Paul Weston (The Bible Reading Fellowship, 2019).

Mountain Moving Prayer by Debra Green OBE with Dave Roberts (SPCK, 2019).

Useful Websites

Here are a number of websites to help resource you and your church in your evangelism.

www.hopetogether.org.uk

www.thegreatcommission.co.uk

www.canonjjohn.com

www.roc.uk.com

www.cinnamonnetwork.co.uk

www.seasonofinvitation.co.uk

www.weekendofinvitation.com

www.trypraying.co.uk

www.theuglyducklingcompany.com

www.ceministries.org

www.olivetreemedia.com.au (Jesus the Game-changer)

www.alpha.org

www.cpo.org.uk

www.zachariastrust.org

For more information about the ministry of Mark Greenwood and to find more information on books, courses and resources visit www.revmarkgreenwood.com

Acknowledgements

A huge thanks to the many people who have made contributions to this book, adding the extra seasoning to bring out its true flavour.

Thanks to Mike Royal, Ed Mackenzie, Andy Lenton, Gary Gibbs and Duncan Logan for your contributions. Thanks to Joanna, Liam, Jason, Zoe, Ron, Ash, Rich, Janet, Luke, Jay, Vicki, Deborah, Linda, Ellen and Neil for writing your faith-journey stories for me to share. They are such a valuable insight into a person's faith journey. Thanks to Roy Crowne and HOPE for allowing me to use the valuable Talking Jesus research. Thanks also to J.John for releasing some of your own research to me for the book.

Thanks to Louise Stenhouse for the hours you spent pouring over the text proofreading and helping it to flow. Thanks to Ashdown Creative who worked their creative magic on the cover and pages, and to Verité for taking it to an actual book.

Thanks to J.John for taking the time to read the manuscript and crafting a wonderful forward and thanks to my many friends who have kindly endorsed the book for me.

Thanks to my wife Emma. This book is the fruit of many of our discussions as together we seek to share about our faith with integrity and sensitivity.

Finally, thanks to all those who have cheered me on in the Big Yes, Little Yes, Healthy Maybe journey, and for encouraging me to put it into a book.